BLUE BLOOD, TRUE BLOOD CONFLICT & CREATION
A Personal Account

By Stewart A. Swerdlow

With Excerpts From
Belief Systems Shattered
by Janet Swerdlow

Expansions Publishing Company, Inc.
P.O. Box 12, St. Joseph MI 49085

Library of Congress Cataloging-in-Publication Data

Stewart Swerdlow
     Blue Blood, True Blood: Conflict & Creation
     A Personal Account
     256 pages
     ISBN 0-9626446-6-8

Library of Congress Catalog Card Number: In Process

DEDICATION

It is with the deepest of heart and soul felt gratitude that I wish to thank my wife, Janet, for her unconditional love and support during my journey through the depths of hell. She was there all the time, waiting for me, and never giving up hope. Without her I would not be here any longer. There are no words in any human language that can express how immensely grateful I am to her for being my twin flame/other half. I have learned brutal lessons these past couple of years. They would have all been in vain if it were not for Janet. Thank you, my true love, from the depths of my being.

There is also a great admiration for my parents and sister who also stayed vigilant during these trying times. They left no stone unturned in exposing the vulgarity and depravity of the demons sent to harm me. I give my wonderful family eternal hugs, and love, and the peace of mind that I shall never be captured again.

As always, my incredible children, who love me without end, have proven to me that there is no space or time that can separate me from them. As they grow into adulthood, I realize that children are a gift that we are allowed to take care of for a while so that the magnificent blossom can grow forth on its own and create a new garden. My children are my jewels and my treasures. Thank you for believing in me.

Finally, I want to thank my fabulous and generous friends who have made my return to my own life easy and happy. Their generosity is overwhelming and their love unforgettable. I am proud to count among my friends: Steve and Sandy Wade, Todd Berran, Lori Sarich, Duncan Cameron, Shannon O'Shea, and Aldee Filley. You have all been as dear family to me.

I also thank you, the public, both readers and students, who have stood by me through better or worse. I am grateful for your continued support and respect. It is my goal to continue to bring you the truth so that your lives may also be healed and that you may experience your personal connection to the God-Mind.

Contents

APPENDICES

Excerpts
Belief Systems Shattered
By Janet Swerdlow

Preface

As far as the history of this planet is concerned, you can consider that everything you ever learned is a complete lie. All history and science books are rewritten to accommodate the agenda of the controllers of this planet. These books are just as false as the New Age material spewing forth from such places as Sedona and Santa Fe, to name a couple of Illuminati meccas. Disinformation is rampant everywhere.

My information comes from my Montauk Project indoctrinations, experiences, conversations with scientists involved in Illuminati programs, communications with alien and interdimensional beings whom I met at various government projects, and through the probing of my own Oversoul.

I cannot offer you physical proof at this time. I can only tell you that it is available in certain places. Although all existence is simultaneous, and time and space are merely illusions of physical reality, for the purpose of this book I will present the majority of history from a linear perspective. There are also infinite universes, both physical and non-physical, but for now, I will only tell you about this one.

To understand how the Illuminati came to power, or even to comprehend what they are, it is important to understand the beginning of life on this world and its progression.

I do not believe in any religion, organized or otherwise. All religions, no matter what they are, are forms of group mind-control designed to manipulate large masses of people to stop thinking for themselves. I do believe in God. It has no religion.

In the subsequent years following the publication of my last book, much has been written about by other researchers concerning Reptilians and their rituals. This theme has found its way into the psyche of the public. Most people are still not willing to accept or even entertain the idea that hybrid Reptilians are in control of this planet and perform blood rituals and ceremonies using humans as the source of food and hormones. I wish it were not true. But I cannot change history, current events, or what I know to be true.

The controllers plan the pattern of coming events in such a way to purposefully disorient the masses while they alone see the destination and the order of life. The masses are lead to believe that haphazard events amidst chaos shape their existence.

In true reality, there is no such thing as chaos. Chaos is simply a pattern not yet understood or perceived. Think about an ant crawling over a designed, tiled floor. The ant may seem confused or disoriented; not knowing which way to go. But a human being watching the ant from a higher perspective clearly sees the floor pattern and knows which way the ant can get to its destination. To the ant, there is only perceived chaos. To the human, there is a prescribed pattern.

To the controllers, the humans are the ants. The controllers are interested in directing the people in such a way that they do not know that they are being directed. The controllers work slowly and methodically from a global perspective to accomplish their goals. With awareness, you too, can perceive order from the chaos, make some conscious decisions, and gain control of your own life and destiny.

1

IN THE BEGINNING...

In the beginning, God existed as a mind and nothing else. All there was, is, and ever will be, is mind. It has no idea where It came from. It only knows that It always existed and has no end. It allows for all thought and ideas to come to fruition somewhere within Itself. It allows any and all events to occur, so in this way It knows Itself. It does not directly interfere with the personal lives of Its thought-creations. It does not have an agenda.

Contrary to popular belief, It does not judge, interfere, or change anything that is already created. It allows for freewill of all creations within Itself. In this way, all possibilities unfold. Nothing is ever stopped from being. Humans may judge events and other beings as good or bad, positive or negative, but to the God-Mind, they are all simply pieces of Itself. The limited human mind cannot comprehend the enormity of creation.

There are many names for this overall intelligence. It is called God, God-Mind, All That Is, Universal Mind, Cosmic Mind, Cosmic Intelligence, Hyperspace, Supreme Being, and The Almighty, among other names. Gender-oriented terms such as Father, Father God, Father-Mother, Him, and His Holiness, are really not appropriate because this intelligence is genderless. Male and female segregation only exists in the divisional physical realities.

This initial supreme energy exists in a hyperspace state with controlling intelligence. I refer to this as the *Language of Hyperspace*, and write about it extensively in my book, ***The Healer's Handbook: A Journey Into Hyperspace (Sky Books, 1999)***. This is a state of being that is pure energy, oblivious to time or space. Here, there is instant transmission of thought and concept. The method of communication is via color, tone, and archetype symbol. This is the foundation of all creation.

In this light, as God-Mind thought about Itself and what It was, thought forms were created that self-perpetuated in creative thought. As this energy became self-aware, all the other forms or levels began to exist simultaneously. All levels of consciousness create the levels underneath them. Like begets like. Each level is supportive and sustains the other levels. This is how existence "breathes." As above, so below.

These thought forms created other thought forms, and so on, and so on. In this way, what is commonly referred to as Christ Consciousness and the Angelic Hierarchy were manifest.

Each manifestation, or level, is equal to every other. Where intelligence is focused gives a perspective to the consciousness. In actuality, all mind and soul-personalities exist at all levels simultaneously. However, lack of understanding and scope prevent full awareness of totality.

Eventually, a circle of creation is formed that feeds back to the original God-Mind, rather than a straight line as commonly thought. This is represented in the toroid shape. This was discovered when the ancient Hebrew language was entered directly into a computer and the Bible skip-sequences were decoded. Those who control this world only allow a fraction of this information released. The ancient Kabalists and members of the secret orders of ancient Egypt and Atlantis knew about this for millennia.

Approximately 5 billion years ago, Angelic-like beings entered into this Milky Way galaxy and attempted to experience life in a physical universe. These Angelic beings who entered into this physical plane quickly became both physical and non-physical simultaneously. The secret government refers to this condition of existence as "extraterrestrial." "Aliens," in government terms, refers to purely physical beings from another physical world in this physical universe. I will use these same distinctions in this book.

Over the 4 billion linear years that these beings existed in this galaxy, they occupied a star system known as Lyrae. This location can be considered the birthplace, or homeland, to all humanoid beings in this galaxy. At this point, the Lyraens had not yet experienced complete corporeal life. They were mostly energetic, physically projecting only when absolutely necessary to experience physical sensations.

At Montauk, we were told that physical beings from another parallel universe entered into this reality and were "guests" of the Lyraens. These guests from the other universe, or "Old Universe," as referred to by the Montauk scientists, enamored the extraterrestrial Lyraens, enticing them to stay increasingly in the physical. Eventually, all of the guests from the Old Universe passed away, but the Lyraens who stayed began remaining so long in the physical that they became trapped in the physical dimension. This is referred to as "the fall from grace" by many traditional religions.

Because the Lyraens were never completely physical, they did not develop weapons. This left them quite vulnerable. Now trapped in the physical dimension, they could no longer use their minds to create whatever they needed. Instead, they had to rely on their bodies to do the work. Their mental connection to their Higher Selves allowed the creation of technology and sustained physical needs. However, the idea of war or violence did not enter into their mind-patterns.

Over linear time, now in a physical state, the Lyraen society became fragmented. The Lyraens segmented into groups with similar mind-patterns. To understand this, use the analogy of a school where the students have clubs based on likes and dislikes. Each of the various groups dress differently, relate to the God-Mind differently, and even develop their own manner of speech and communication. All of this breeds segregation rather than unity. Segregation leads to weakness and lack of cohesion, which in turn leads to vulnerability. When the links of a chain are made of different material, the chain can be more easily broken.

2

THE TRANSPARENT PEOPLE

When I worked at Montauk, I encountered an occasional alien species known as a "Reptilian." They seemed to pop in and out of physical reality. The Reptilians primarily use the lower astral realms as their reference point, or point of entry, into physical reality. This is the origin of the legends of astral demons. My Montauk controllers explained that these beings were brought to the Draco star system eons ago by another group unknown to anyone. Further, they explained, no one knew anything of their true origins.

When I was about sixteen years old, I discovered the truth about the Reptilians. I was living on central Long Island, and had been in the Montauk project for about two years. My bedroom was on the second floor of my parent's home. My sister's room was down the hallway. From her bed, and through her open doorway, she could see my bedroom door.

One night, I "awoke" in my bed to see a strange creature standing by the side of my bed. About six feet tall, it had a whitish pallor to it. I could see right inside of its body. I saw veins and arteries, and what looked like internal organs all pulsating inside. It did not have any external gender definitions, but I sensed that it was predominantly male. The head was featureless except for the brain that I saw inside of its skull area.

Communication with me was entirely telepathic. Mentally, it told me that it came from the far future where humans no longer existed, and that its species was not from this reality. Continuing, it said that its species had traveled back into the distant past to create a race of beings, which I knew as the Reptilians, to antagonize and test humans.

It also told me that they were assisted by the Sirians of Sirius A in the creation of the Reptilians and their placement in the Draco star system.

The Sirians are creations of the Ohalu Council, another non-physical group of beings. The Sirius binary star system was never part of the Lyraen civilization, nor was it ever colonized by them.[1]

Finally, it told me that I was one of its species who voluntarily entered the Earth plane to help humans and the Reptilians deal with each other.

The being left my room by walking out of my bedroom door. I fell back to sleep. The next morning at breakfast, my sister told me that she saw the weirdest thing the previous night. She could not sleep, and glanced down the lighted hallway to my bedroom door. She said she saw a transparent being come out of my room, walk briefly down the hallway, and vanish! She said you could see right through it! My heart sank in my chest. I told her about my experience. Neither one of us said another word. In fact, we never discussed it again until only recently.

Through the following years, these beings kept in occasional communication with me, mostly telepathically. I called them the "transparent people." The interesting thing about that term is the word "parent." These transparent people are not physical in our sense of the word. They are like an energetic mass that can segment part of itself to communicate with denser beings like humans. Think of them as a sea of conscious energy that exists outside of time and space, but can tap into any physical or non-physical reality that they choose.

I was indoctrinated by them as well as by my controllers and handlers. I now believe that my overseers knew about the transparent people, and wanted information about them through me. When my soul-personality was transferred into this body from Johannes von Gruber,[2] the Sirian in charge of the transfer was fully aware of the needs of the transparent people, and placed some of their collective consciousness in me.

When the transparent people created the Reptilians in the astral plane the Reptilians were borderline physical. The transparent people cannot really enter into the physical dimensions because their energy vibratory rate is so high that it cannot sustain a physical body. So when they appear, it looks like a transparent glass shell.

For the Reptilians to function in physical reality, they needed physical genetics. The transparent people took genetics from the now physical Lyraens, who had blonde or red hair, and blue or green eyes. These genetics were mixed with the transparent people's collective energy, thus manifesting physically as the Reptilians. This is why the current Reptilians need the energetics from "Aryan-type" people to survive on the physical plane.

Once the Reptilians were created in the astral, they needed a physical home base from which to accomplish their task. For this, they were taken to many different physical realities in which they could become the dominant species. Mentally, they were programmed to conquer and absorb all of the races and species that they encountered. Those that could not be absorbed were to be destroyed. The purpose of all of this is to determine the most perfect form in physical reality that can exist in any environment. Think of it as a gigantic, cosmic "Survivor" contest.

The Reptilians are programmed to believe that they are the superior physical form. Scientifically speaking, Reptilian DNA does not change very much over eons of time. It basically remains the same. For them, this is their proof that they are already perfect, without any need to adapt.

Mammalian life, on the other hand, evolves and changes form constantly to survive. To the Reptilian mind, this denotes weakness and inferiority. Reptilians are also androgynous, meaning male and female in one body. This is comparable to all non-physical forms that have no gender...like God-Mind. For this reason, the Reptilians believe themselves to be more godlike because of their androgyny. Due to their ethnocentric values, they also consider it their right to control and conquer all of space and time.

Although the Reptilians operate out of a general group mind, they are separated into seven different Reptilian species, each created to perform specific functions.

This is their hierarchy, and is based on the nine level Angelic Hierarchy that I discussed in *The Healer's Handbook: A Journey Into Hyperspace* (*Sky Books, 1999*). As an aside, the Hindu caste system is a direct replica of the Reptilian hierarchy.

---

[1] There are rumors in the artificially created New Age movement that Sirius is actually a trinary star system. This is totally false. Three stars revolving around one another would create an energetic field that would pull them into each other, thus destroying them. There can be no physically sustainable model for such a system.
[2] Refer to *Montauk: The Alien Connection*, (*Sky Books, 1998*)

3

IS THIS PLANET TAKEN?

Because the Lyraens did not have a defense system in place, they were a sitting target for the Reptilians, also referred to as the "Draco." After being brutally attacked by the Draco Empire, the survivors of the Lyraen society dispersed to other locations throughout the galaxy. The remnants of the Draco attack on Lyrae are still seen by today's scientists. In 1985, a newspaper article stated that scientists are able to observe remnant waves of a blast that fan outward, and emanate from a central part of this galaxy. They believe this blast to be several million years old and of such intense proportions that the wave is still traveling toward the edge of the galaxy before dissipating They claim not to have any idea of what created the blast.

These survivors went to Orion, Tau Ceti, Pleiades, Procyon, Antaries, Alpha Centauri, Barnard Star, Arcturus, and dozens of other solar systems. In this solar system, the refugees colonized the planet now called Mars. At that time, it was the third planet in the solar system. A world called Maldek was the fourth planet in this solar system, and was also colonized.

The Lyraens were all blonde-haired, blue-eyed people, with an occasional red-haired or green-eyed person. In Lyraen society, red-haired people were considered special with extrasensory powers that connected them to non-physical realms. They were especially desired for breeding purposes. Special permission to breed with a red-haired person was required because of the extra, or superhuman, abilities that came with the offspring.

For this reason, red-haired people were kept separate from the rest, and even had their own subculture. They were also coveted by the Reptilians, who as a species, did not have much psychic ability. Often, when Reptilians came to a world for occupation, the Lyraen refugees offered a group of red-haired people to appease them for a while. This practice eventually degenerated into sacrifices to appease the demons.

The planet Earth in those days was a water world in second orbit from the sun. There was little land above the surface. The only intelligent inhabitants were an amphibian race that was completely without technology. The atmosphere of the Earth was mostly liquid. The planet definitely could not sustain any type of human life forms.

The dispersed Lyraen descendents developed their own cultures over the eons of time. Even their genetics manifested differently as a result of the mind-patterns of each of the colonies. For instance, Mars and Maldek were similar to the current Earth environment, with warm to temperate climates and an oxygen-rich atmosphere. The gravity on Maldek was denser than Mars, so those people developed a thicker frame and a more aggressive attitude.

Eventually, skirmishes developed between the occupants of the two planets. Mars was rich in resources. The people of Maldek thought that they deserved these resources for survival. The Martians asked the beings of Sirius A, from the planet Khoom, for defense technology to shield their planet from attack, not only from the Reptilians, but from their humanoid neighbors and cousins. The Sirians are known throughout the galaxy as merchants of technology. They have the best, even sharing it with the Reptilians. So, the Sirians created a defense mechanism located in the Mars underground.

Mars is a hollow planet, as are Earth and Jupiter. Planets created with material ejected from a star have hollow interiors. As a molten ball is thrown from the star and starts spinning away, it begins to cool. The centrifugal force of the globe spinning and moving at great speed pushes the molten interior to the sides, forming the crust of the planet. This, in turn, forces hot gases out of the poles to form openings at both ends. The molten core and gases that remain get trapped between the hollow interior and the plates below the crust of the globe. These are pushed out periodically in the form of volcanic activity.

The nexus point on any such globe is always at the 19th parallel of the planet. It is evident on Earth by the Hawaiian volcanoes, located at the 19th parallel; by the Mons volcano on Mars located at the 19th parallel; and at the red spot on Jupiter, also at the 19th parallel.

The geometry built into the monuments on Mars by the Sirians and Lyraen colonists explains about the 19th parallel through its geometric equations and measurements. This geometry is also replicated and contained within the Giza Plateau in Egypt.

4

THE REPTILIAN AGENDA

The Reptilian agenda was, and is, to seek out the human refugees for destruction or assimilation, and to use their blood and hormones for sustenance.

The remnant Lyraens who colonized other planets formed an alliance against the constant Reptilian attacks. They called this alliance the Galactic Federation, comprised of 110 different colonies. The colonies belonging to the Federation wished to maintain their new identities, and no longer associate with the old way. Together, the Federation colonists managed to repel the Reptilian attacks.

There were three primary groups who did not join the Federation. These three groups were considered extremists, or nationalistic idealists, seeking to recreate the glory of the old Lyraen civilization. One group was the Atlans, located on a Pleiadian planet. The Pleiades actually consists of thirty-two planets orbiting seven stars. At that time there were sixteen different colonies of Lyraen descent throughout the Pleiades. These colonists all wanted to oust the renegade Atlans because they remained independent and did not assist their human cousins.

The other two groups were the Martians and Maldekians, who were already at odds with each other. For this reason, the Reptilians turned their attention toward this solar system with its two human colonies. In the Reptilian's estimation, it would be easy to divide and conquer.

The Reptilians love to use comets and asteroids as weapons and ships, using them to travel through the stars. First, they create a small black hole as a propulsion system that pulls the larger planetoid towards its destination. When used as a weapon, they use a particle beam accelerator to create a blast that hurls the comet or asteroid to its target. All of the technology was obtained by the beings from Sirius A.[1]

In this way, they hurled a huge ice comet aimed at Mars and Maldek. The Reptilians, not being very technologically oriented, miscalculated the trajectory. The pull of the gigantic gas planet, Jupiter, pulled the comet off course. The ice comet then headed directly for Maldek. The citizens of that planet asked the Martians for help. Even though they were at odds with each other, they allowed some of the Maldekians to move to the Martian underground. The comet came so close to Maldek that the planet got caught between the gravitational pull of Jupiter, Mars, and the comet. This caused the planet to explode, leaving an asteroid belt between Mars and Jupiter. [2]

The explosion pushed the ice comet close enough to Mars to rip the atmosphere off that planet, leaving only an extremely thin atmosphere. The explosion also pulled Mars further away from the sun

The comet then continued on toward the Earth. The heat of the sun and the gravitational pull between the two globes forced the watery atmosphere of the Earth to polarize. This polarization pulled most of the ice from the comet to the polar regions of the Earth, thus covering most openings to the inner Earth, while at the same time exposing huge land masses for the first time.

The comet then switched places with Earth, taking up the second orbit from the sun, becoming the planet now known as Venus. The heat of the sun melted the ice on the comet, creating a cloudy covering to this new planet. The Earth was pushed out to the third orbit occupying the previous position held by Mars. The Earth was now ready to be colonized. Most of the surviving amphibians were transported to a new home on Neptune. Some stayed in the newly formed oceans.

The Reptilians who were inside the hollow comet, now Venus, came to the surface of this new world. They built seven domed cities, one for each of the seven groups in the hierarchy. In the mid-1980s one of New York's daily papers, *Newsday,* reported that a Soviet space probe penetrated the cloud layer of Venus and photographed seven white domes the size of small cities, all in a row. After a page-long diatribe, the American scientists concluded that this was all a natural formation.

The Reptilians drove a large, hollowed out object into Earth's orbit to begin the colonization process. This object is now called the Moon. Conventional science considers the Moon natural, yet it is the only known object in space that does not spin on its axis. The Moon faces the Earth in the same position all of the time, leaving one side in complete darkness. A sonic resonance sent to the surface of the Moon makes a pinging noise like a hollow object. If the Moon were solid, the noise would sound like a thump or thud. The Moon is hollow. A recent article in an astronomy magazine said that the Moon was being reclassified because it is considered to be hollow.

The Reptilians chose a large continental landmass to begin their civilization on the Earth, now referred to as Lemuria or Mu. This was a vast area in what is now the Pacific Basin, extending from Japan to Australia, and from the coast of California to Peru. The Hawaiian Islands are in the middle of this one-time landmass.

Here, an androgynous Reptilian culture developed. They brought with them the creatures that were their sustenance - the dinosaurs. All beings create beneath them animals and plants that are a reflection of the mind-pattern. Reptilians create dinosaurs, humans create mammals. They are not designed to coexist on the same planet.

Additionally, the thinking process of the Reptilians differ from the human thinking process. Because Reptilians do not evolve rapidly and remain unchanging, their expansion is also slow-moving and insidious. It would take several millennia for the Reptilians to decide whether or not they would coexist with humans. After all, Earth was still an outpost far from the center of the Draconian Empire.

In the meantime, the Martians were now living underground with their hostile Maldekian guests. Something had to be done quickly to prevent them from destroying one another. So, the Martians petitioned the Galactic Federation to remove the Maldekian refugees to another planet. The Galactic Federation also received a petition from the Pleiadian Council at the same time, asking the Federation to remove the Atlans from their star cluster.

The Federation thusly decided to use the Atlans as a counterbalance on Earth. If the Atlans survived, the Maldekians would also be sent. The human/Lyraen descendents were literally throwing their own riffraff to the Reptilian colonists on Earth. In this way, the Federation would get rid of their undesirables. The undesirables would occupy the attention of the Reptilians. The Federation would gain valuable time to build their own forces against the Reptilians.

When the Atlans arrived on the Earth, they colonized what became known as Atlantis. Their continent stretched from what is now the Caribbean Basin to the Azores and Canary Islands, as well as several small island chains reaching up to what is now the East Coast of the United States, including Montauk Point.

The industrious Atlanteans rapidly grew to a large, prospering civilization needing more territory. The dinosaur population was rapidly increasing and becoming dangerous to the human colonists. The Atlanteans began destroying the dinosaurs to protect themselves. This did not sit well with the Reptilians. Soon major battles occurred on the Earth between the Lemurian Reptilians and Atlantean humans.

At the same time, the Maldekian refugees arrived on Earth. They created a large human colony in what is now the Gobi desert, northern India, Sumer, and other parts of Asia.

The Maldekians attacked the lunar surface where the Reptilians guarded their Earth outpost from invasion. The Maldekians also bombarded Atlantis and Lemuria with laser weapons. The dinosaurs were wiped out.

Additionally, the Martians also attacked the Reptilians from space since they, too, were searching for a Reptilian-free environment in which to live. This might be considered the real First World War on this planet. It was a mess!

---

[1] The Sirians were at war with the Orion system. This hostility exists to this day. It is intriguing since the beings in Orion were once very human, as Lyraen colonists, and then were taken over by the Reptilians. However, the Sirians and the Reptilians trade with each other and the beings from Sirius A sell weaponry to the Dracos! A complex political situation indeed.

[2] The comet also caused the planet Uranus to flip on its side. It is the only know planet that rotates north-South instead of East-West.

5

CONFLICT & CREATION

To stop the fighting and make the Earth peaceful enough for colonization, a meeting was held by a council from the Andromeda Galaxy, on a planet called Hatona. This meeting took place outside of the Milky Way Galaxy with a neutral council because all civilizations within the Milky Way Galaxy were in some way connected to the fighting, and all had some sort of stake in belonging to the winning side.

The Hatona Council convened for many decades as the fighting continued in this solar system. Finally, with their intercession, an agreement was reached between some of the human factions and the Reptilian Earth colonists. Keep in mind that this agreement was without the participation of the Reptilians from the original Draco Empire.

The agreement stated that a new breed of humanity would be created on Earth that would contain the DNA of all interested parties who participated in the "peace" process. A designated area on Earth would be set aside for the creation of this new species. The Earth-based Reptilians of Lemuria agreed to this under the condition that the Reptilian body be the foundation for this new being. This is why the original Bible states, "Let *us* make man in *our* own image." This is a plural statement because it was a group project.

To achieve a new species from a Reptilian androgynous body, it was necessary to separate the genetics into male and female components. This is the allegorical story in the Bible of Adam and Eve. Creating Eve out of the rib of Adam is actually the story of separating the androgynous Reptilian body into male and female. This is why all humans on this planet have Reptilian DNA with Reptilian traits. This is also why human fetuses go through Reptilian-style development in the womb before looking humanoid.

Many prototypes were developed over millennia. Under the supervision of the Hatona Council, races were created and then destroyed when it was not acceptable by all parties. This explains why ancestors of mankind appear and then suddenly disappear in layers of archeological analysis.

Twelve humanoid, and one Reptilian, groups donated DNA for this purpose. Mankind was developed in the area now known as Iran/Iraq, as well as parts of Africa. Hybrids were also developed on Atlantis and Lemuria. Remnants of these are seen today as the Bigfoot or Yeti in North America and Asia; the aborigines of Australia; and the pygmies and Watusi in Africa.

The African versions were created by beings from a nomadic, artificial planet known as Niburu, or Marduk. These Reptilian-like beings travel in a manufactured world looping our solar system. The Sumerians called them Annunnakki.

The cosmic joke to this project is that all of the groups donating DNA secretly programmed sequences to cause their genetic strand to be predominant. This set the precedent for eternal conflict. Humanity was doomed to fight and be controlled. No one group would ever be in charge. The project was doomed for failure before it even began!

Such DNA programming invites tyranny and oppression. Soul-personalities attracted to such a planet have a victim mentality. Many advanced cultures call Earth a prison planet, and dump their criminals here as punishment. Once in a while, one of these soul-personalities reveal themselves, such as Richard Dahmer, Charles Manson, Richard Speck, and Vlad the Impaler (Count Dracula), to name a few.

The Reptilians ensured that the new Man would be forever attached to the Reptilian frequency because the foundational prototype was Reptilian. This meant that the new Man could easily be mentally controlled by them.

Upon discovery of this information that the Reptilians wanted control of the new race, the Atlanteans began a severe electromagnetic bombardment of Lemuria. This bombardment caused the bulk of the continent to submerge into the ocean, now called the Pacific Ocean. The only parts left above the water are the Hawaiian Islands, the California coast west of the San Andreas fault, Australia, New Zealand, the South Pacific Islands, Japan, the Philippines, Taiwan, and the islands of southeast Asia.

The Reptilian survivors went to Northern India, the Earth's interior, the planet Venus, and parts of Central and South America. Inner Earth became the "homeland" for most of the surviving Reptilians of Lemuria.

Here, they created a vast underground civilization. This started the legends of hell and demons living in fire under the Earth. They built tubes containing fast, subway-like vehicles that can travel to any point on the Earth within a few hours. They created the famed underworld cities of Akkadia, Agartha, Hyperbolea, and Shamballa that are sought by explorers to this very day. These cities are built along the inside wall of the inner crust that lines the interior of the Earth. Remember, the hollow Earth is not a theory, but a scientific fact caused by the cooling and spinning of a planet as it is ejected from a star or sun.

The primary entry points to the inner Earth are via the North Pole, where there is an opening of 1300 miles, and the South Pole, with an opening of 950 miles. These can be seen from space. That is why commercial aircraft are not allowed to fly over these areas; not because of magnetic disturbances, which is the "official" reason. Admiral Byrd reported on these openings in the 1920s until his information was concealed by the government.

At the very center, or nucleus, of inner Earth, there is a globe of energy left over from the creation of this planet that acts as an inner sun. It is the light from this object suspended by gravity and centrifugal force that causes the light of the aurora borealis.

Numerous cave entrances to the inner Earth exist in the Rocky Mountains and Sierra Mountains in the western United States, as well as less numerous openings in the Ozarks and Appalachian Mountains. Entries also exist in the Alps, Himalayas, Andes, and the Caribbean. There are also numerous suboceanic entry points, particularly in the deep trenches of the Pacific Ocean, the Caribbean Sea, and the Atlantic submarine mountain ranges especially on or near the Azores, Canary Islands, and the Falklands.

All of these areas are closely guarded by local governments and N.W.O. elite forces. Artificially created entrances exist under the new Denver airport, the Giza Plateau in Egypt, major Air Force complexes around the world, and many of the Temples in India and China. A major Chinese entry point is under the Shensi Pyramid that is out of bounds for everyone in Western China.

Of course, with the Reptilians off the Earth's surface, the Atlanteans were free to "play" with this new mankind and establish humans as the ruler of this planet. They established colonies all over the remaining portions of land. They invited the Sirians to "come and play" with them. They booted the Marduk beings off-world and took control of their slaves. They created new hybrids for sea and land, one of which became the Merfolk, a genetic blend of human and dolphin. The dolphin species was brought here from the Andromeda Galaxy to monitor all of these events.

Whenever the Atlanteans detected underground Reptilian activity, they blasted the inner Earth with lasers and electromagnetic pulses to kill them. Unfortunately, this weakened the upper crust of the Earth's top mantle riding over the trapped magma between the upper and lower crusts. After several millennia of these attacks, the Atlantean continent started to break up. Their civilization began to break up as a reflection of the physical deterioration of their continent. The Atlanteans became even more belligerent as fear and destruction overtook their mind-patterns. Black magicians and sorcerers took the place of scientists and religious leaders.

Fortunately, the population foresaw the destruction that was coming. Many refugees relocated to what is now Egypt, Peru, the Appalachian mountains and western Europe, just before the continent collapsed into the upper crust of the Earth. This collapse caused the Earth to flip on its axis, creating the legend of the Flood written about in the Bible, and in other world cultures.

This catastrophe was used as a window of opportunity by the groups that donated DNA to create mankind. They immediately began "reorganizing" the humans into new groups that became the basis for future nationalism. The Sirians helped to create the ancient Egyptian culture. Those from Tau Ceti organized the Slavic culture. The Rigelians were busy in China and the Orient.[1]

While all this was transpiring, the Reptilians saw an opportunity, and seized it!

[1] Refer *to Milky Way Galaxy* chart

6

BLUEBLOODS!

The inner Earth provided a subterranean locale for the Reptilians to regroup and formulate plans to retake the surface. At this point, the Reptilians were completely cut off from their home in the Draco constellation. Their spaceship, the Moon, was in human hands. They were alone, isolated on a now hostile planet. They needed to defend themselves.

They developed a plan to insidiously retake the surface by blending their genetics with the genetics of the surface humans. Because the human prototype already had Reptilian genetics, it was easy to access the mind-pattern. The Reptilian frequency was already established in the brain stem as well as the Reptilian brain section of these hybrid humans.

The population of Sumer was chosen as the starting point. These humans were primarily descendents of the Martian, Maldekian, and Lyraen refugees. The Reptilians have a preference for the genetics of blonde-haired, blue-eyed people whose mind-patterns and genetics are so easily controlled. They abducted members of the ruling classes, including political leaders.

Using these humans, they began a new hybridization program that took several generations to perfect. Their goal was to reach a human/ Reptilian genetic 50/50 split. This would produce a human-looking Reptilian that could easily shapeshift from Reptilian to human, then back again. Shapeshifting was accomplished simply by concentrating on the genetics the hybrid wished to open, or lock up, whatever the case may be.

For this program the Reptilians engaged the help of the Sirians who had the technology to implement such a program. The Sirians knew a lot about genetic alterations and mind-programming, which they freely shared with the Reptilians.

Once the hybridization program was complete, the Sumerian leaders were now shapeshifting Reptilians. The new Reptilian hybrid became the elite of that culture. Their blood, because of the increased Reptilian DNA, contained more of a copper content. Since copper-based blood turns blue-green upon oxidizing, these Reptilian hybrids were called "Bluebloods."

The Bluebloods quickly realized that with a 50/50 human/Reptilian genetic split, it was necessary to intermarry to maintain the 50/50 split bloodline necessary to shapeshift. When the split increased too far to the Reptilian side, shapeshifting became difficult, and holding human form became impossible. In these cases, it was discovered that the ingestion of human hormones, flesh, and blood, allowed the Reptilians to maintain the human form.

Human form was necessary to maintain to avoid scaring the population, which was now not accustomed to the Reptilian form. Control of the masses was easier when the orders came from a humanoid. The Reptilian format was kept to religious icons and legends. The statues of their gods and goddesses reflect the Reptilian influence, even showing a female Reptilian holding a hybrid baby.

The shapeshifting Reptilian Bluebloods asked the Sirians for help with the daily maintenance of their human forms. The Sirians determined that feeding the hybrids human hormones and blood in an altered animal form would be the easiest way to do it unnoticed by the population.

The sacrificial animal used by most Middle Eastern people was the wild boar, so the Sirians chose it as the basis for this new animal hybrid. Human genetics were mixed with those of the wild boar to create the domesticated pig. This animal was served daily to the Bluebloods as a method of temporarily maintaining their human form until they could use an actual human in a sacrificial ceremony.

Because the domesticated pig is a combination of human and animal genetics, eating it is a form of cannibalism. This explains why the Hebrews considered it unclean to eat. This is also why the pig is considered to be the most intelligent animal on Earth, why pig skin can be grafted directly onto humans in burn cases, and why pig heart valves can be used in humans with little difficulty. Cancer drugs and other chemicals are often tested on pigs before humans.

The domesticated pig frequency, or group mind, is the perfect vehicle for animal species to enter before entering human form on their evolutionary progression. In many respects, pigs can be considered a form of humanity. To a lesser degree, the same is true about cats.

As time progressed, the civilization of Sumer declined and transformed into other cultures. Vast migrations from Sumer to other locations in Central Asia occurred. The migrating peoples took their Blueblood leaders with them, as they were their royalty and kings.

The Sumerians became known as the sum-Aryans, or just, Aryans. They spread out across Asia into the steppes of Russia and into the Northern Indian subcontinent. In India they encountered the dark-skinned Dravidians, who were Reptilian remnants from Lemuria. The Dravidians were driven to the central and southern parts of India, while the Aryan hybrids took control of the north, and into the foothills of the Himalayas. The Aryan leaders, all Bluebloods, became the Sultans and Rajas of legend and history. Sumerians also created Babylonia.

The Sumerians also migrated to the area known as the Caucasus Region, where the Khazars developed. From the Caucasus Region, the Blueblood kings and their people spread west toward Europe, developing into the Franks, Cambrians, and Teutonic nationalities. These nationalities were also being manipulated by various alien cultures like the Antarians, Arcturians, Aldebarans, Tau Cetians, and other remnants of the Lyraens, such as the Atlans. The Atlans located here eventually became the Celts.

To back-track for just a bit, I had said in a previous chapter that the descendents of the Reptilian hybrid Sumerians went into Central Asia and the Middle East. They mostly established themselves in the Caucasus Mountains and became the Khazars. From here, they spread west toward Europe, seeding the national identities for the Vikings, the Franks, the Teutonic peoples, and the Russians. Keep in mind that when Atlantis sank, some of those refugees went to western Europe and developed into the Celts. Some went to Greece and others to the Italian Peninsula. These peoples were here before the hybrids moved in. It was during the interim time period from the destruction of Atlantis until the Sumerian descendents moved in that other alien groups started to add their genetic mix to the pot and develop individual cultures based on their home worlds.

These Blueblood leaders also infiltrated the Middle Eastern peoples, such as the Biblical Canaanites, Malachites, and Kittites.

At the same time in Egypt, the Sirians were reorganizing the Atlantean descendents there, known as the Phoenicians. The Phoenicians were blonde-haired, blue-eyed, with some green-eyed, red-haired people among them. The Phoenicians colonized the coastal Middle East and the British Isles. They even colonized parts of the Northeastern North American continent, all the way to the Great Lakes area. Some of their mines and writings on stone tablets can still be found in the woods of North America.

The Sirians were also genetically creating the ancient Hebrews. The Jewish people are actually a combination of these genetically manipulated Hebrews and the Sumerians. These Jewish people were then released into the Palestinian territory. The name, Palestine, comes from the ancient people, the Philistines, who were actually Phoenicians.

All of these mixed in the coastal plains of Palestine and created a new religion based on sacrifice and an avenging alien controller, that they called God, or Elohim.

Similarly, when the Aryans mixed with the Dravidians in India, they created the Hindu religion, which is actually a recreation of the Reptilian seven-tier hierarchy. The caste system of India is a direct copy of the Reptilian division of function.

At the same time that all of this was going on in western and central Asia, the Rigelians, were developing the remnants of Lemuria who escaped to the coast of eastern Asia. The Rigelians were a human civilization that was controlled, and eventually assimilated, by the Reptilians. The Rigelians assisted the inner Earth Reptilians in developing a hybrid that included Rigelian DNA. The Rigelian/Reptilian hybrids set up dynasties in what is now Japan and China that developed independently of their western cousins.

In their mania for control, the Reptilians used the various races that donated DNA to the original human project. They fastidiously monitored these related sections of hybrids to determine which was best suited for overall control, and which for subservience. All the hybrids could be controlled through the Reptilian brain that hooked them into Reptilian mind-patterns, but some were more controllable than others.

In Europe, the Bluebloods insidiously took control of the various tribes and groups, becoming their kings and royalty. They infiltrated the Arcturian experiment, called the Etruscans and started to create a new global empire through the Romans. These European Bluebloods then entirely eliminated the Antarian experiment in Greece, and instigated their plan for globalization through the Roman Empire.

The Reptilians even offended the Sirians by infiltrating the Egyptian experiment and implementing their religion there.

The Reptilian hybrids became like the endometriosis of the known world, slowly growing into all areas and creating control through the Blueblood system.

7

OTHER ALIEN GROUPS

While the Reptilians were the first colonists on Earth, they were not the only ones who interfered with human development on this planet. In all there are twelve other groups who donated DNA to the production of the experiment. Add the Reptilians to the twelve groups, resulting in human beings with a genetic mixture of 13 different strains.

The result was a general free-for-all. While all these humanoid aliens were Lyraen/Reptilian descendents, each group was culturally and physically manipulated by different groups. This is similar to a lab professor who leaves the door open while he is gone, and all his assistants add their own genetics to the experiment.

The Tau Ceti aliens centered their attention on the eastern European area, from what is now Serbia to the slopes of the Ural Mountains. From here, they influenced the Slavic and Russian peoples. The geographic conditions resembled that in the Tau Ceti star system, and its colony Epsilon Eradanus. The Tau Ceti added their DNA to the human prototypes that were already established there, creating what is now known as the Slavic peoples. The results were a race of humans who were stocky, barrel-chested, and averaging 5'6" to 5'9" in height, with a dense bone structure and dark eyes. They were aggressive, and preferred a cold climate.

These Tau Ceti/humans were virulently against the grey alien race and the Reptilians, because their worlds had been attacked, and their children stolen and killed by both races. The Tau Cetians vowed to follow the grey race and destroy them.

In the 1950s, the Soviet Union signed an agreement with the Tau Cetians to use bases in Siberia and under the Ural Mountains. For this reason, the city of Sverdlovsk, named after my great-uncle, the first president of the Soviet Union, was closed to outsiders. Many experiments involving radiation on the public were performed here from 1958 through the 1980s. A United States spy plane was shot down over Sverdlovsk in the early 1960s when the United States was trying to learn about the secret activities taking place there.

In central Europe, the German tribes were genetically manipulated by beings from Aldebaran. These people are very intelligent and scientifically-oriented. They are generally blonde-haired and blue-eyed, with a minority of dark-haired, light-brown to hazel-eyed people. They are militaristic, and prefer to keep to themselves. For almost 2,000 years, the Aldebarans have been energetically connecting to the Germanic peoples, telepathically sending information to them and promoting a national sentiment.

Many humans of the Aldebaran frequency have mixed with the Tau Ceti descendents in the Slavic area, particularly in Poland and Russia. Hitler knew this. That is why he was so adamant about invading those countries and incorporating them into his empire. Hitler was only half Germanic. His father was a wealthy Jewish businessman in Austria. His mother worked at the home as a maid. She had an affair with the master of the house, and when the wife found out about it, had the maid thrown out. The Jewish businessman did nothing to help Hitler's mother. For this reason, Hitler hated the Jews and sought to destroy his own genetic lineage, basically because he hated himself. He was also deeply mind-controlled.

The Aldebarans also genetically infused the Vikings. These Nordic people inherited the aggressive and militaristic tendencies that are also seen in the Germans. The Vikings plundered and raped across Europe for centuries, but did not have the technological ability to stay in power.

An accidental manipulation of genetics occurred on the Italian peninsula 3000 years ago. A ship from the Arcturus star system crashed landed on Etruscan territory. These humans were actually extremely spiritually-minded, and instead of trying to get back home, stayed and blended into the humans of that part of Earth. Their descendents became the Romans who were then infiltrated and mixed with the central Asian hybrids.

Beings from the Antarian star system were behind the genetic manipulation of ancient Greece. These people were a society predominantly based upon homosexuality. Females were used for breeding only. In fact, there were Antarian observers at the Montauk Project who were interested in the programming aspects of sexuality as they related to the Wilhelm Reich methods. The Antarians are dark, often with olive skin, dark eyes, and short, thin bodies. They have a fabulous musculature due to the density of their home-world, and are known for their body-building goals.

The Greek-Antarians colonized Spain and Portugal. Their descendents further mixed with the Romans, and Arabs who are predominantly Sumerian/Reptilian. These then colonized Central and South America, mixing their genetics with the native Indians who were of Atlantean-Procyon descent.

The Procyon star system does not have much technology. The Procyons were brought to this planet after the fall of Atlantis to boost the survival rate of the refugees. They became the Maya, Aztec, and Inca. They were given ancient Lemurian and Atlantean outposts in the Andes and Sierras of Mexico. They tried unsuccessfully to recreate these cultures, including emulating the building of the pyramids, performing medical procedures, and finally, sacrificing to the Reptilian gods. This is why their legends speak of blond men returning in chariots from space to take them away.

The Anasazi Indians of the American southwest were also brought from Procyon. It was the Sirians who so generously provided transportation. The Sirians even attempted to bring the Hebrews to the American west. Ancient Hebrew coins were found in New Mexico and other parts of North and South America.[1]

Over the millennia and recent centuries, movements of nations, colonizations, war, and famines, have thrown the Earth's population into a giant melting pot. Strands of genetics have continuously mixed with one another, especially in North America, Europe, Australia, the Caribbean, and South America. The result is that there are few pure races left, and the racial and cultural unity makes it easier for group control.

While all of this was going on in Europe and the Middle East, the Chinese Empire was expanding over East Asia, and the Dravidian-Reptilian culture in India was being replaced by the Aryan (Ari- and Sum-Arian) hordes from Central Asia. In South America, the Inca Empire was flourishing as it was mixed with the genetics of the Procyon star system.

The same mixture was happening in North and Central America creating the Toltecs, Mayans, and Aztecs. All of these cultures used blood-ritual and human sacrifice. This indicates that the Procyonians were themselves conquered by the Reptilians and did their bidding, even though they were humanoid. All of the Central and South American cultures used snakes and Reptilians as symbols. These people have a unique blend of Lemurian/Draco and Atlantean/Human genetics mixed with the Procyonian DNA.

[1] For further details of the flow of genetics and alien intervention in mankind, please refer to the *Milky Way Galaxy* chart in this book.

8

THE CRYSTAL SKULL

When the Hatona Council convened to determine the development of life on Earth, they pondered two questions. First, if the Earth beings were left to develop on their own, how would they know their true origins, and second, if there was no interference, how could they be prodded in the correct direction.

One E.T. group that was primarily non-physical decided to leave a repository of knowledge for those who evolved enough to understand it. These muscular beings were tall with golden-bronze skin, golden hair, and violet eyes. On an etheric level, this E.T. group created an object that contained within it the sum total of knowledge of the Mind of God as they knew it. They also programmed this object with the history of the universe and all the technology that would ever be necessary.

For the object this group chose the shape of a female human skull without any racial features. The skull represented all humanoids, symbolizing brotherhood and harmony. The female was chosen because it was to be placed in physical reality as a symbol of ego being overcome. Crystal was chosen because it represents the highest vibration possible in physical reality—purity, clarity, focusing, and magnification. The movable jaw piece symbolized the fact that it was a communication device. The E.T. group left the Crystal Skull with the first Lyraen/ Atlantean civilization where it was placed in a temple pyramid to be energized by the Lyraen/Atlanteans over many aeons of time.

When the Sirians infiltrated the second-generation Lyraen/Atlantean civilization, they negotiated with the Atlans to study the Crystal Skull. Over time, they created an exact duplicate that they brought back to

Sirius A. Other alien groups made inferior copies of it for use with their own human creations. By the time the third generation Lyraen/Atlanteans were well established, the true purpose of the Crystal Skull was almost entirely forgotten.

Those in power tried to use it for negative purposes, not realizing that this magnified and reflected back all their evil deeds and intentions. In addition, the Crystal Skull was created in such a way that whatever is thought in its presence reflects back, becoming a part of the thinker's experiences. The Crystal Skull teaches that the physical universe mirrors thoughts.

When Atlantis sank, high priests fleeing the continent brought it to Central America to where the Procyonians brought the Maya. Here, it was used as an object of worship and reverence until the Maya were removed from the Earth. Eventually, the Crystal Skull remained buried in ruins until its discovery in the early part of the 20th Century, when the Crystal Skull allowed itself to be discovered.

The Crystal Skull operates through the trinity of communication - color, tone, and archetype. When any combination of these three is beamed or thought of in the presence of the Crystal Skull, it opens a program that is coded to a particular frequency resonance.

An infinite number of combinations can be used, and any one will unlock a program in the Crystal Skull to teach mankind. The left-brain represents language, and the right-brain represents pure thought. The pineal gland of communication balances and translates the left- and right-brains with the use of archetypes.

Archetypes can be geometric shapes, letters, numbers, Ancient Hebrew symbols, pictograms, or any combination of these. Colors are also part of the triad with a language all their own. The left-brain is dark, the right-brain is light, and once again, the pineal gland balances and translates this through colors. Tones also represent the trinity of sound, balancing music and silence. In the same way, the Crystal Skull balances the Mind of God and physical reality.

At times, the Crystal Skull becomes non-physical. Because it was created without a body, this symbolizes the needlessness of the physical body. The Crystal Skull is a bridge between all levels of reality. Anyone who knows the sequences of the trinity of communication becomes all-powerful and omniscient.

9

THE ANCIENT HEBREWS

Most modern Jews have absolutely no genetic link to the Middle East. There are in fact, many different physical types of Jews, covering many racial characteristics. This supports the fact that they are not a homogeneous group, but a religious group that spans many cultures. The story of Abraham going out from the city of Ur and coming to Canaan is really telling the story of the Reptilian hybrids leaving Sumerian territory and colonizing other parts of Central Asia and the Middle East. The vast majority of European/American Jews can trace their genetic lineage to the Khazars, mentioned in the last chapter, who all converted to Judaism in the 800s to circumvent the Catholic rule of the Holy Roman Empire.

In the year 2000, the University of Pavia in Italy did a genetic study of European men. They found that 80% of them had a direct lineage to Central Asia and the other 20% to the Middle East. This supports the statement that the Sumerians entered into Central Asia and then migrated to Europe and the Middle East. This also nullifies the theory of Africa as the birthplace of mankind. There is absolutely no genetic connection from Asia or Europe to Africa.

The ancient Hebrews have nothing to do with modern Jews. As mentioned in the previous chapter, the Hebrews were Sirian-created in Egypt by combining Sirian and Lyraen genetics. These people were tall and powerful, and spoke the Sirian language which is the equivalent to the ancient Hebrew language. Scholars agree that the Hebrew language suddenly appeared on the scene.

The ancient peoples of Palestine spoke Aramaic, which was the parent language of Arabic, Farsi, and several other Middle Eastern dialects. Originally, Hebrew was a language used exclusively by the priesthood and the Egyptian secret society. Eventually, ancient Hebrew began to mix with Aramaic, among other languages.

The Hebrews were actually paid workers in Egypt. They were sent to Canaan to assimilate the native cultures for the Egyptian Empire. They mixed with the local tribes of Sumerian-hybrid descendents, practicing blood-ritual and human sacrifice. All of this was incorporated into a conglomerate religion based on ancient Egyptian/Atlantean/Sirian beliefs. That is how Judaism was born.

The story of the Exodus of the Jews from Egypt is a poor retelling of the destruction of the island of Santorini in the eastern Mediterranean Sea by volcanic explosion. The lava dispersed into the sea causing it to turn blood-red. The volcanic ash and rock that spewed forth created the legend of the plagues on Egypt. Many citizens fled the area. The Red Sea parted when the ground under the water rose up, exposing land that could then be crossed. Several hours later, it sank back down, drowning whoever was still trying to cross.

The actual translation of how the Ten Commandments, or the Bible codes, were transmitted to the people of the Exodus, states that the people spontaneously started speaking the instructions. This is a demonstration of mind-to-mind communication. In this case, programming was electromagnetically activated, revealing DNA instructions that were then written down. These instructions were designed to keep the experiment/ project in line.

The Middle East became a focal point for the Sirians and their Reptilian allies. Together, they generated a new version of religion and culture for ease of global control and domination. What better way to do that than by programming a race of nomadic people that would carry the religion and culture everywhere on the Earth.

Whenever the conditions within the experiment became unmanageable, the particular overseer group made corrections. For example, most people are familiar with the story of the cities of Sodom and Gemorrah, where a group of humans in the mankind experiment went awry. Their sexual habits were not conducive to propagation since they were predominantly homosexual.

A virus was introduced into the population to destroy it. However, it started to spread outside the immediate region. This disturbed the controllers, so they sent two agents to investigate, and to determine if anyone was salvageable. The local inhabitants called them angels, because of their blonde hair, blue eyes, and perfect bodies.

Lot and his wife took the agents into their home to protect them, since all the men in town wanted to have sex with them. Soon after, Sodom and Gemorrah were destroyed. To this day, radiation can be detected at the site. Melted rock is seen in the canyon walls. Sodom and Gemorrah were eliminated with a nuclear weapon.

In the early 1960s, Israeli scientists digging at the site of Sodom found remnants of bone and body tissue encased in rock. American scientists were called in because they had better equipment. What they found in the preserved body tissue was a sample of the virus. The Americans reconstituted it with living cellular nuclei. Quietly it was tested on a terminally ill patient in a St. Louis Hospital in 1967. The man died a horrible death. The virus was called AIDS because it removed whatever immune system the man had left. The American research determined that this thousands-of-years-old virus was artificially genetically created.

The ancient Hebrew religion was a conglomeration of the Sumerian-Reptilian belief system, ancient Egyptian-Atlantean-Lyraen belief system, and the Reptilian tribal subcultures found in the land of Canaan that were incorporated into one acceptable dogma. It included blood-ritual and human sacrifice, which is why Abraham was so eager to please God by killing his own son on an altar. This symbolism came in handy later on for religious purposes.

The Hebrew language itself did not appear until after the Hebrews left Egypt, and then only for religious ceremonial purposes by the priests. In fact, many of the terms and names used in the Hebrew religion came from the Egyptian ceremonial rites. The name, Moses, originates from the title given to adepts of the secret Egyptian pyramid cult. This Egyptian ceremonial title, Moshe, means "he who is anointed with crocodile fat from the Nile River."

This ceremony was performed inside the King's Chamber in the Great Pyramid. In Hebrew it meant "out from the water," in reference to the crocodiles. The Egyptian word for crocodile fat, was Messeh from which the term Messiah is derived. To be anointed with crocodile fat rendered into an oil, was to absorb powerful, unchanging Reptilian energy and assimilate this into the body. Moshe, or Moses, was a ritual title, not a person's name and was a reference to the crocodile fat used in temple and pyramid ceremonies.

A leader such as a Moses was a logical choice to spearhead a migration of people to safety from a place of turmoil, such as when the destruction of the island of Santorini, also known as Thera, blew up and created havoc on Egyptian territory, causing many to flee. It would also make sense for the Sirian controllers of Egypt to send out their genetic creations, the Hebrews, to a place of safety in the Sinai desert like a safekeeping until needed.

It was then that the Torah, or Holy Commandments, was given to this people as a code by which to live. This document is in a code that can only now be deciphered with the use of a computer. The land of Canaan needed to be conquered in order to give development room to the new creations. In effect, the Hebrews were the next sequence of the experiment, and the old versions were to be eliminated or assimilated.

The Hebrews carried the new coded laws in the Ark of the Covenant (Coven of Ants), that only the priests could touch. When the University of Minnesota in the 1960s attempted to build the Ark as described with instructions in the Bible, it was so electrically charged that it had to be dismantled! This is why the ancient Hebrew priests entered into the Ark area alone, for safety reasons. They also had to wear white linen, as non-conductive clothing, and wore a special breastplate that grounded them electrically and acted as a protective shield. The Ark was really a communication device. This is why the priests had "messages from God" whenever they were in the Ark's presence.

The Ark also acted as a location device for beacons originating outside of this planet. The Ark was originally kept in the Great Pyramid to focalize energies. It was sent with the Hebrews for safekeeping. It has since traveled from Egypt to Canaan/Israel to Ethiopia, back to Israel, and now is located under the pyramid again. However, there are actually two Arks. The second one is in Jerusalem.

10

THE ANNUNNAKI & THE BLACK RACE

The creators of the black race, the Reptilian beings of Marduk known as the Annunnakki whose planetoid travels in an elliptical orbit of this solar system every few thousand years, are due to arrive in 2003.

The Annunnakki like to develop slave races for specific purposes, creating them out of lower animal forms. In the case of their Earth creations, they used simians to create a slave race to work the mines in what is now known as Africa. This race was genetically designed to work and live in hot, humid conditions with a limited life span. Diseases were programmed into them to prevent development of culture, and cause them to become dependent on their creators for existence. This is why in the genetic memory of all other races, the blacks are slaves.

The American and European Illuminati decided to use the AIDS virus as a weapon to remove the black race from Earth. These Illuminati concluded that if the Blacks were no longer here, the Annunnakki would find the condition of their slaves unacceptable, and not interfere with Illuminati plans. The green monkeys of east Africa were subsequently infected with the AIDS virus, along with the blood supply of Haiti. In Africa, AIDS is a heterosexual disease. The World Health Organization, WHO, was also used to directly inject the AIDS virus into the population under the guise of immunization.

However, a "monkey" wrench turned up in the plans. A gay French-Canadian flight attendant had sex with a bisexual partner in Africa. The infected flight attendant angrily spread the disease wherever he went. New York City and San Francisco were two of his primary destinations. He alone is determined to have been the main carrier outside of the intended target. The Illuminati does not think of everything.[1]

By 2003 when Marduk returns, most of Black Africa will be infected. Those who are not infected will be killed via Ebola, war, or famine.

Most Caribbean and North American blacks have a high percentage of European genetics that are not considered desirable for slave purposes.

In 1999, newspapers reported that US astronomers said that a huge planet had been detected beyond Pluto with an elliptical orbit opposite to all the other planets in this solar system. They said it was on a trajectory that would take it to near the Earth in 2003! Not another word was printed about it after that.

The remnants of the Marduk/Reptilian experimentation in Central and Southern Africa were basically left on their own. The beings from Marduk, the Annunnakki, also known as the Abbennakki, left the Earth, continuing on its elliptical journey through the solar system and beyond.

This artificial planet passes near Earth every 12,000 years. A complete orbit takes 24,000 years. The last time they passed Earth, approximately 10,500 BC, its gravitational pull exerted in conjunction with Atlantean crystal experimentation, caused the Earth to flip on its axis, sinking Atlantis.

The Annunnakki/Abbennakki have robotical scout ships that monitor Earth when the artificial planet is not close. These ships have a crew of workers that look like dwarfed bears. They are known to be aggressive, even attacking humans in the past. These bear-like creatures are cyborgs with brain implants that allow control from a distance. Their bodies are organic and powerful.

These creatures started appearing in the late 1960s. Government-released UFO investigation reports document their existence. More of these creatures will be seen in the next two years. Stay away from them! They are dangerous.

Most likely, they will surface in Africa to check on the Black race for their masters on Marduk. Louis Farrakhan, the Black Moslem Leader, has often spoken about his UFO contacts. According to Farrakhan, these contacts explained that the Black race was created by them. They further told him about the need for the Blacks to develop without interference from other races.

---

[1] This was augmented by experiments on gay men in New York City under the guise of Hepatitis shots.

11

MIND-CONTROL VIA RELIGION

The first religion on Earth was the Reptilian belief system brought by the colonists of Lemuria. Their religion believed in a God-Mind that contained a hierarchy, or caste system. This caste system was extrapolated to the several Reptilian species incorporated into the Draco Empire. Each species had its own place in the structure of their society. Every individual knew its functions and respected these boundaries. To violate these rules meant death.

The Reptilians operate as a group mind, meaning that no single Reptilian can make a decision for itself. Only the upper caste, or winged ones, have the semblance of individuality. They were, and are, the leaders.

When this religion was brought to Sumeria, the caste system was infused into society as a religious hierarchy. Remember that the colonists of Sumeria were refugees from Lyrae/Mars/Maldek. They, like the Atlanteans, maintained the original belief system of the Lyraen culture. The Lyraen belief system encouraged individuality, as well as promoted service to others as a pathway to self-growth. The Lyraens believed that red-haired people were connectors to God-Mind, and as such, used them as oracles.

The Reptilians worshipped the transparent beings from the astral planes as their creators. The transparent beings have a mass consciousness, like an Oversoul. They are basically genderless, although in terms of physical reality, their characteristics and traits render them more masculine than feminine.

When the Reptilians brought this religion to the Sumerians, they were careful to introduce it in a way that would be accepted and followed. First, they created a gender base for a gender-minded population. Then, they instilled fear to control the mind-patterns. Cleverly, they devised a religion based on a male-female, god-goddess control system. The male

43

god was called Nimrod; the female goddess, Semiramus. They are depicted as half-human, half-Reptilian. Their appearances were designed to frighten the humans into submission.

Nimrod and Semiramis eventually became the Osiris and Isis of Egypt, and the Apollo and Athena of Greece, among many other gods. All used the male/female, god/goddess theme because it represented the original Reptilian androgyny and the separation of the human prototype into the male/female, Adam/Eve.

Because of the "masculine" tendency of the transparent people, and despite being androgynous themselves, the Reptilians prefer the powerful male over the female. They represented their androgyny in Sumer by placing three horns on the Reptilian God, Nimrod. There are many layers of symbolism to this:

- The penis and two testicles.
- Two energies uniting to create a third, i.e., the human prototype.
- The three levels of existence: hyperspace, astral, and physical.
- The three levels of awareness: conscious, subconscious, and superconscious.
- Androgyny leading to male and female sections.

Thus, the number three was an important symbol to the Reptilians on Earth. They represent this in many ways, including the lily, or fleur-de-lis with its three points. They also use the scorpion with its stinger and two piercing claws.

The advanced version of the scorpion is the eagle, which represents the scorpion in its higher form. Because of this, the eagle came to represent raising from a lower form to a higher one. It represented power and globalization. Because it was a bird of prey, it was able to capture everything beneath it, especially live food. For these reasons, the Romans always used an eagle on their staffs whenever they marched into a city or country.

Most people do not realize that all birds are descendents of Reptilian dinosaurs. Many corporate logos and superheroes of today have wings attached to them. The wings also represent the winged Reptilian leaders in the upper echelon of the Reptilian/Illuminati flowchart.

Half a continent away in China, the remnants of Lemuria created a male-dominated Empire system. Here, the male Emperor would always have an Empress. The people were told that the Emperor and Empress were descendents of the Sun-God. The symbol of the Empire was the dragon, another Reptilian figure. This "royal" family created a dynasty that ruled tight-fisted for millennia.

The Chinese Reptilian religion spread across Eastern Asia, while the Sumerian version meandered through Central and Western Asia. The spread of these religions was intentionally controlled from the underground Reptilian population, primarily centered under Tibet. Looking at a world map, one can easily see that this is the best underground base location in Asia to reach all areas of the continent. These Reptilians were aided by beings from Sirius B who developed the Buddhist philosophies, as well as a group of renegade Lyraens trying to reproduce a Lyraen civilization under Reptilian control. Strange bedfellows!

At the same time in India, the Lemurian Reptilian refugees created a caste system that was a direct replica of the Reptilian hierarchy, from the lowly workers/untouchables to the Brahmin/winged ones. This Indian/Reptilian culture remained localized, writing the ancient Vedas and building temples to the various Reptilian gods.

Meanwhile, the Egyptians, who were Atlantean/Lyraen refugees, were in the process of building a new civilization from the remnants of their two major ancestral ones that were destroyed. The beings from Sirius A helped them, as they were a major factor in the interactions of Atlantis.

As previously stated, in Egypt, the Reptilian gods were known as Osiris and Isis. The Egyptian panacea of gods included a large variety of hybrid creations, half-human, half-animal. This was reminiscent of the Atlantean hybrid experiments that found their way into Egyptian culture, and was promoted by the Sirians who were preparing that culture for a Reptilian takeover.

The Atlanteans were so entrenched in the original Lyraen belief system, that it took several millennia for the Reptilians to get a stronghold in that culture. Now that the remnants were scattered over the Earth and non-cohesive, it was easy to send in infiltrators (in-full-traitors) to sway the belief system toward a Reptilian flavor. This began with the introduction of the cat as a focal point of worship.

In the Sirius A star system, the main world is called Khoom. The ancient name for Egypt is Khem. There is also a correlation with Mexico. Some researchers say that the Bay of Campeche translates to the Bay of Old Egypt, indicating a connection between Egypt and the Yucatan Peninsula. This is not so. Sirians who interacted with Atlantis named this area after their home world, and then carried the name on to the new refugee culture in Egypt.

Another planet in orbit around Sirius A is a world called Kilroti. Here, the Sirians created high-intelligence cat-like beings. These cat-like beings are called the Lion People. In the 1970s and 1980s, the government created a cartoon for children that described these beings.

In the high astral levels, there is an etheric race of Lion Beings who are gold, have wings, and violet eyes. The name of the race is Ari. Ari is also the old Hebrew word for lion. Their frequency is more powerful than the dolphin frequency. The Ari created the Ohalu Council that governs the Sirius A star system.

The Kilroti were generated by mixing the genetics of the Sirians with the energy of the Ari. This is what was brought to ancient Egypt. As the non-physical energy descended into physical reality, DNA formed that could be used to create corporeal life.

This was then mixed with human and wild lion DNA to form the common house cat found on Earth. The cat was given to every home in ancient Egypt, and programmed to leave at night to report back to their alien controllers. This is why cats to this day have the urge to go out at night. This also explains their aloof nature.

The Sirians incorporated worship of the cat idol into the Egyptian religion to ensure the perpetuity of this method of spying. The Sirians also built the Sphinx as a symbolic reminder of the blending of human genetics with lion frequency. This was a way to energetically bind future civilization to the Sirians. The Sphinx was designed to face the morning star Sirius A every day. The face on the Sphinx is identical to the face on the Mars monument that looks down to the Earth at the Sphinx.

Sirian technology built the complexes at the Cydonia plateau on Mars, upon the arrival of the first Lyraen refugees. The new Martians were unaware of the close Sirian connection to the Reptilians.

The original pyramids, built after the destruction of Atlantis, were energy points. They were the same shapes underground as above, making them into octahedrons. At their center is a tetrahedron. This master shape is the archetype symbol for God-Mind totality. Anything at its exact center is absolutely protected. The octahedron is also the shape of the Delta-T antenna used at the Montauk Project. This shape, when energized in the proper color codes, causes interdimensional rifts, creating vortices and wormholes. Rituals performed at this center point produce vast energies that can be transmitted through hyperspace to anywhere in creation.

Some researchers claim that the pyramids were pumping stations for underground Nile tributaries. This is only partially true. Because water is an electromagnetic amplifier, it was used to surround the ritual chamber located in the Delta-T to boost ritual energy. Using these methods, the ancient Egyptians controlled weather, destroyed enemies, created stargates, and boosted their Reptilian energies in ceremony. This is also why the Montauk Project was located near vast amounts of water.

The Great Pyramid is part of a protective solar system grid, linking the Moon and Mars monuments together to produce a force field to repel invaders. The Great Pyramid is also connected to other points on the Earth such as Stonehenge, a submerged Atlantean crystal, Tiahuanaco, Ayers Rock, and the White Pyramid in western China. Together, they form an energy containment field similar to an electric fence. The HAARP project in Alaska taps into this.

Meanwhile, a dynastic culture similar to the Reptilian Chinese dynasties was forming in Egypt. The Reptilian control religion based on Osirus and Isis fanned out over northeast Africa and the Middle East. At the same time the Reptilian Sumerian cult of Nimrod and Semiramus fanned out over Central Asia.

A unification of these beliefs was necessary to accomplish the plan set forth from the beginning. This is why Abraham originated in the Sumerian city of Ur, journeying westward toward the Middle East. It was no accident that the followers of Abraham wound up in Egypt, where the Sirians then created the Hebrews. The Hebrews were destined to be the cultural prototype for the future world. This is why they were programmed to wander all over the Earth and influence all existing cultures.

With all of this as a background, the Reptilian Bluebloods now needed to form a global empire that would encompass the cultures that they had inspired. They needed to counteract the other alien groups that had been working diligently in Europe to create more human civilizations.

12

THE ROMAN EMPIRE

Another important alien group was the Arcturians. They came later, mixing with the Etruscans who then created the Roman civilization. The DNA of the Etruscans was altered to become dominant and aggressive. The Arcturians believed that this was the only way to counter the Reptilian hordes. There is an ancient story that says Rome was founded by the twins Romulus and Remus, who were born from a wolf mother. The wolf is the symbol for clan. The wolf is also a mammal, representing the human origin of the culture. Here again was an attempt to recreate the Lyraen civilization on Earth.

However, the influx of the Sumerians changed all previous plans. As soon as they entered Europe, the hybrids began to interbreed and occupy the various territories. Their goal was to reach Rome, and take over that culture before it spread too far. This goal was accomplished when the Reptilian/human hybrid immigrants from the region of Troy, reached Italy. Here, one of the males married the daughter of King Latinus, who started the Latin culture in Europe.

As the Roman civilization grew, it began to incorporate the various other national identities around it, particularly along the Mediterranean. Rome occupied most of Europe as well as the Near East and into North Africa. The Roman civilization picked up where Egypt and Greece left off, in another attempt at globalization.

Ancient Greece is rarely written about these days. This is because the Antarians were anti-Reptilian, and promoted homosexuality as part of their culture. The Reptilian/human hybrids promoted bisexuality and heterosexuality due to the balance of energies and the use of sexual magic with it. The Greeks were human-oriented, attempting to spread their culture globally as well. However, their culture did not allow for sufficient population increases to accomplish their goal. Therefore, they were easily assimilated into the more powerful Roman Empire.

With their Reptilian mindset, the Romans had a specific agenda to conquer everything. In addition, they were difficult beings with which to deal. They demanded strict obedience to their rulers and the Reptilian hierarchy, and severely punished violators. They used the eagle as their symbol because it commands everything below it, preys on weaker species, and like all birds, descends from Reptilians. Astrologically, the eagle is the higher form of the scorpion, which easily kills its enemies on the ground.

The Romans rarely incorporated other customs into their own. Instead, the Roman culture was simply imposed on the occupied nation. This type of influence promotes resistance. As the Roman Empire increased, imprinting the mind-patterns of its conquered nations, it became apparent that there was a need for an underlying unification to link these various cultures together.

13

EMMANUEL

At this time, a Federation of Lyraen-descended worlds was forming at the center of the Milky Way Galaxy. These were the same group of blonde-haired, blue-eyed people and red-haired, green-eyed people that destroyed Sodom and Gemorrah after the AIDS virus ran rampant there. This was the group of people who sent the "angels" that appeared to Lot and his wife.

With Sirian cooperation, they were working to gently push the post-Atlantean remnants back into Lyraen culture now that the Reptilian hybrids were taking over. Of course, this isolated Lyraen group did not realize the current treacherous Sirian Earth involvement. When someone is friends with everyone, they really are friends with no one.

The primary purpose of this group was to thwart the insidious Draco. Unbeknownst to them, the Sirians were taking advantage of both sides. They were helping a messianic prototype to be under Reptilian control. Toward this goal, they were creating a prototype for the next phase of human development. This group abducted a young woman from ancient Israel with extremely pure humanoid genetics, implanting her with a fetus genetically designed for a specific purpose. Today, this woman is known as Mary, and this is why it is claimed that she was a virgin.

Some authors and researchers now claim that Jesus never existed, and that the entire New Testament was fabricated. Others claim that Jesus existed, but say that he was a political activist whose feats and miracles are misinterpretations of ancient Hebrew or Aramaic terminologies. Both schools of thought are simultaneously correct and incorrect.

These people are also either willingly or unwillingly being used by the Illuminati to undermine current world religions. The Illuminati eventually plans to replace current world religions with a new world religion that will have to be followed by everyone.

51

There really was a Christ figure on the Earth at that time. Personally, I know this as fact because one of my jobs at the Montauk Project was to go back in time and extract a vial of blood from his body.[1]

There was a persona named Emmanuel. He was a product of the mixture of Mary and a Lyraen descendent. Mary was physically abducted and implanted. She said that she was visited by angels. As a young man, Emmanuel was removed from his mother, and taken to the Great Pyramid on the Giza Plateau. Here, he was taught ancient Lyraen/Atlantean/ Egyptian principles for twenty years.

He was also taken aboard the Federation ships and indoctrinated in ways to steer the masses away from the Reptilian influences. His orders were to inculcate the three strains of humanity that had the purest Ari-an genetics on Earth. These were the Hebrews, created by the Sirians; the Germanic tribes, created by the Aldebarans; and the Northern Indian Ari-ans who now lived in the foothills of the Himalayas. All three peoples used a lion as their symbol, and were descendents of the original blonde-haired, blue-eyed Lyraens.

Most of this information can be found in a 2,000 year-old, resin-encased document uncovered in Jerusalem by a Palestinian researcher. This researcher translated some of this document, now called *The Talmud of Emmanuel*, into Swiss German. This manuscript is no longer available in the United States, and is difficult to find even in Switzerland. The Illuminati had the Israelis murder the Palestinian researcher who found the document before he finished deciphering it.

It is true that the New Testament has been completely altered. The New Testament was rewritten to support the Roman Empire claims of superiority, as well as to change the perception about God and mankind. The Pisos, a Roman family related to one of Rome's Emperors, were commissioned to rewrite vast sections of the Bible. They were instructed to make the masses feel unworthy and lowly, and to eliminate any reference to their true heritage as spiritual beings.

Sections relating to reincarnation, aliens, the true creation of Emmanuel, and the true story of the crucifixion were completely removed. The sections dealing with the Apostles and the heritage of humanity were completely changed to allow for a "slave" mentality to occur. The Romans decided to use the cross as the symbol for Christianity because in ancient Hebrew, the word for cross is Tslav. This is a linguistic homonym for the Latin esclavo meaning, "slave." The first influx of Christianity came from the eastern part of Europe, moving westward from Israel and Greece. Those people were called "Slavics" because they followed the sign of the cross, and were slaves within the Roman Empire.

The entire crucifixion scenario was staged. The Christ figure was drugged before being placed upon the cross. Then he was removed, revived, and shuttled off to India by way of Damascus. His mother went with him, and he lived for a very long time. His grave can be seen to this day in the city of Srinigar, in the province of Kashmir, a hotly contested territory between India and Pakistan. The grave is tended by a Jewish family. There are researchers who dispute this claim in order to nullify the importance of the true history of Emmanuel.

In the hills of the lower Himalayas, the small villages have legends and histories concerning Emmanuel, who sojourned there for many years. These stories say that he lived until the age of 117, when he "gave up" his body. The villagers do not believe he really died then either. Many people in remote Himalayan villages report that he bleeps in and out of physical reality at will, and is able to literally manifest such things as food and clothing out of the air.

This was reported to western civilization in the late 1800s and early 1900s by a researcher and his entourage who stayed in the area for a couple of decades, and wrote a series of books on the subject. In fact, this researcher lectured all over the United States before he died in the 1940s. His research encouraged Hitler to send teams of explorers to the area in the 1930s. The researcher, Baird T. Spalding, reported on time travel technology and magical events associated with the appearances of a Christ-like being.

The doctrines of Emmanuel are very different from the Jesus of the known Testaments. He encouraged self-analysis, and said that material gains were fine as long as one received them honestly. He said that lesbianism was acceptable, but stated that male homosexuality was not because it wasted genetic material. Emmanuel married Mary Magdalene and had three children with her.

Current New Age disinformation states that Emmanuel was from the Order of Melchizadek. The Order of Melchizadek did not exist at that time because that was a political office, nothing more. Melchizadek comes from the Hebrew words, melech tzedech, which means "charitable king." Melchizadek was a title bestowed on the director of the Sanhedrin in Jerusalem. The Sanhedrin was the court system that made laws for the people. The holder of this title also acted as an advisor to the king. The title of Melchizadek was passed down from father to son.

Emmanuel criticized the holder of this title, accusing him of corruption. For this, Emmanuel was ostracized. This placed him, his children, and Mary Magdalene in physical danger. Mary did not get a long with the Apostle Peter and did not want to stay in Israel. The crucifixion was staged as a way to secrete the entire family out of Israel to a safe place. Emmanuel went to India with his oldest son to remove some of the danger from his family, and also because he was being placed under Reptilian control. For the rest of the family going through Central Asia was too difficult for them, so they were sent by boat across the Mediterranean to an area that was hilly and fertile, yet difficult for the Romans to occupy due to local resistance.

Mary Magdalene and her two youngest children, along with Joseph of Arithamea, Emmanuel's brother, set sail for the South of France.

---

[1] Refer to my book, *Montauk: The Alien Connection (Sky Books, 1998)*.

14

MAGDALENE LINEAGE & BEYOND

Mary Magdalene and her entourage arrived in the South of France in approximately 30AD. Emmanuel/Jesus was born in 6BC, rather than in the year 0 as commonly reported, and on the Spring Equinox of March 20th.

Even today, the residents of the small coastal villages in the area on the western-most portion of the French Mediterranean coastline re-enact the arrival of these "holy" travelers every year.

Mary Magdalene took her crew up north into the hilly countryside. They actually lived in a series of caves that are common in the area. Her children grew to adulthood and also married. Joseph of Arithamea went with some of his men to the British Isles where they set up houses of worship and spoke about the Christ figure. They enshrined in Britain many relics from Emmanuel that today are in the possession of the Windsor family.

The caves in which Mary and her family lived are now covered by a castle in the town of Rennes-Le-Chateau. Much mystery surrounds this place, especially the rumors that it contains massive secrets pertinent to Christianity. The secret is that is sits over the entrance to a large cave network, much like the cave networks found in the American Ozarks, which is an entry point to the underground Reptilian world. Most of the private and mysterious castles and churches in Europe sit on top of such entry points. These entry points are common in the South of France, Bavaria, central Switzerland, and in the Pyrenees.

The grandchildren and other descendents of Emmanuel did well in the following three centuries. They married the children of the leaders of the area, maintaining their Hebrew identity. In fact, for a couple of centuries, a large area of Southern France was a Jewish Kingdom.

These genetics mixed with the Celtic/Atlantean genetics that were already present.

There was a reason that Mary chose France as a place of refuge. It is commonly known that of the original twelve tribes of Israel, ten were missing from Ancient Israel. This goes back to the time when interference by other alien groups was in process in Europe and they were adding their own blend to the mix.

They decided to use the Sirian-created stock from the Hebrews to mix with the Celtic/Atlantean since they trusted the Sirians in their efforts to recreate Lyraen civilization. The missing tribes were taken elsewhere to enhance the cultures in Europe and the Americas.

The Aldebarans took the tribe of Dan to Germany. The Danube River is named after them. The Federation took a group of tribes to Scotland and off shore islands, which are named The Hebrides. Ancient Hebrew coins have been found in the desert of New Mexico, and ancient Hebrew words have turned up in the languages of South American Indian tribes. The Hebrew Talmud describes underwater bases where strange grey creatures took the Hebrews as a staging area. The Hebrew Bible talks about giants in the Earth as well as people under the Earth. Skeletons of giants are turning up all over the planet. Does modern science or history have any rational explanation for this? No!

In attempt to unify this conquered area as well as remove resistance, the Roman Empire decided to assimilate it. Declaring itself the "Holy" Roman Empire, it adopted Christianity as a global religion and installed the Vatican in Rome. At this point in the 300s AD, the Reptilians were in full control of Rome.

The only problem was the Magdalene lineage to the west which still needed to be assimilated The descendents of Mary Magdalene had developed a huge following, and created their own culture, mixing with the Franks, Cambrians, and Castillians. The Magdalenes had also intermarried with the children of the Merovee lineage in France, to be known as the Merovingians. Their symbol was the bee, a creature with a hive mentality, where each works for the greater good of the collective.

So, instead of feeding the Christians to the lions, the Roman Empire used the lion as one of its primary symbols! In this way, the Reptilians merged with the lion people. The new symbol for this new hybridized group became the Reptilian lion, now seen on every family shield in the European Blueblood elite lineage. Today in Europe, almost every building has some form of a Reptilian-lion appearing on a plaque or flag. Most coat-of-arms display this, as well as the Reptilian fleur-de-lis symbol.

All of the royalty and wealthy elite of Europe and the Americas claim descent from this combined lineage. The Vatican uses it as leverage to control governments and corporations. The current Pope is an Illuminati loyalist who in his youth sold Zyclon B gas to the Germans in WWII to help the extermination process. This network of deceit and control pervades the ruling classes.

Once the Holy Romans achieved this coup of total influence in their known world, they began to spread even further into parts of Central Asia, the British Isles, and North Africa. This became a problem for the Khazars in the Caucasus area because the Khazars were in control of the trade routes between Asia, Europe, and the Middle East. They were not interested in paying taxes to the Vatican, or the Christian Romans. Even among the Illuminati elite, there is dissention. Each faction wants to be the one supreme command.

To escape control of the Holy Roman Christians, the entire Reptilian-Khazar-Babylonian-Sumerian sector converted en masse to Judaism in the 800s AD. Then, to infiltrate and control their own European brethren, these now Jewish immigrants established footholds in the west, including Russia, Germany, Poland, and Bohemia which eventually became Czechoslovakia and Hungary.

Babylon was the civilization that Sumer developed into as it expanded into Central Asia to become the Khazars. In fact, many of the Blueblood organizations that developed through the millennia called themselves Babylon Brotherhoods. The Babylonian Brotherhoods later combined with the secret Atlantean-Egyptian schools in Europe to become the Freemasons. Some of these immigrants went by the name of Bauer, now known as the Rothschilds. This family quickly took control of the financial and trade foundations of Europe.

To equalize things for their eastern cousins, this influx from Khazar prepared the way for the Mongolian-Reptilian hordes to march toward Europe, mixing their version of genetics into the existing gene pool. Genghis Khan and his Empire controlled more of the Earth than anyone in history up to this present day. His control stretched from East Asia to Eastern Europe, and down through central Asia. This was a brilliant maneuver by the Reptilians, equalizing the various controlling factions, instead of polarizing them into subgroups that would weaken the power of unification and the overall agenda.

Those of the Aldebaran frequency, not willing to be outdone, sent the Viking genetics all over Europe and North America. Even prior to the arrival of the Vikings in Greenland, Canada, and the northeastern

United States, the Phoenicians, who were Atlantean refugees, settled areas around the Great Lakes. Here, the Phoenicians mined pure copper for weapons and trade. Many of their cuneiform tablets are still found in outlying areas of Michigan, Minnesota, and Wisconsin.

The Mayans also established settlements in the Great Lakes area to extract minerals and herbs, sending them back to Central America. Mayan mounds can be found all over the United States' Midwest, as well as a pyramid that is at the bottom of a lake in Wisconsin. The Mayans and Phoenicians were trading partners with common territory in the Great Lakes region.

After the consolidation achieved under the Holy Roman Empire during the Middle Ages in Europe, it was necessary to divide the power base amongst the hybrid Reptilians. This was important to successfully control the Earth's resources without creating conflict among the ruling classes. Territories were carefully created, each one with a "royal" family at its helm to which the masses were expected to pay homage.

As previously stated, the hybrids maintain a 50/50 DNA split between human and Reptilian energies. This enables them to shapeshift between human and Reptilian form. This manifestation is controlled by the mind-pattern. A Reptilian mind-pattern manifests the Reptilian features. For this reason, the hybrids intermarried amongst the 50/50 elite group, thus ensuring the perpetual control of Reptilian shapeshifters over the others on the planet.

Whenever these genetics deviate from the required 50/50 split, it is hard for the hybrids to maintain the human form. When this happens, it becomes necessary to intermarry with a subgroup of elites containing a higher human mixture, for example, a 40/60 split, to thereby balance the next generation. This was one of Princess Diana's purposes.

Genetic breeding problems in this time period created some elites with an excess of Reptilian DNA, making it difficult for them to hold human form. To counteract the problem, the hybrids used a preponderance of blood rituals. Because of this, legends of vampires flourished. Stories of vampires turning into bats was a misinterpretation of the elites who shapeshifted into winged Reptilians during ceremonies.

One such legendary individual, Vlad the Impaler, lived in the Transylvania territory between Romania and Hungary. He was known for his "blood and mutilation" parties in which many poor young townspeople became his dinner.

Meanwhile, the greys, a mix of human and Reptilian genetics, started creating beings for the sole purpose of blood and hormone extraction from humans and animals. Then, they brought these biological substances back to the greys. This further perpetuated the vampire legends.

In Central and Southern France, legends of the loupe-garou, or werewolf, were also forming. Remember the story of Romulus and Remus, the founders of Rome who were born from a wolf mother. This is more than simply a symbolic story. The Atlanteans were famous for their genetic experimentation. To them, wolf energy symbolized the epitome of male mammalian virility and power. They created half-man, half-wolf creatures as guardians of the scientific temples, and used them in sexual magic rituals.

After the destruction of Atlantis, these creatures became known as the Anubis in Egyptian deism. As a result of the sexual rites, many females were impregnated by the Anubis. Their progeny who maintained a high percentage of wolf genetics had the unfortunate ability to shapeshift into werewolves. Mary Magdalene brought some of these people in her pilgrimage to the South of France.

There are also hybrids with bear genetics. The original group of bear-humans was released in the high mountains before Atlantis sank. These hybrids are known as Sasquatch or Bigfoot in North America, and Yeti in the Himalayas and Siberia. There are pockets of them in various other locations.

There are also the lion people, whose genetics were discussed in an earlier chapter as well. There are humans walking the Earth now who contain a small percentage of these animals within them.

15

THE ILLUMINATI HIERARCHY

The leader of the Earth's Illuminati is called the "Pindar." The Pindar is a member of one of the 13 ruling Illuminati families, and is always male. The title, Pindar, is an abbreviated term for "Pinnacle of the Draco," also known as the "Penis of the Dragon." Symbolically, this represents the top of power, control, creation, penetration, expansion, invasion, and fear. The holder of this rank reports to the purebred Reptilian leader in the inner Earth.

Recently, there are reports that the Marquis de Libeaux is the Pindar, but this is disinformation. The true current Pindar is the head of the Rothschild family, as has been for several hundred years. He is based in Germany near Frankfurt. In the late 1970s, he oversaw the sister project to Montauk, called M.A.L.D.A. is an anagram for Montauk-Alsace-Lorraine Dimensional Activation. This project was located near the city of Strasbourg, France, historically once part of Germany.

Interestingly, there is a winery on the east end of Long Island, not far from Montauk Point, called Pindar Vineyards. This wine is growing in popularity, gaining international accolades. This fits nicely into the plan, as this area will be a part of the capital district of the Earth/United Nations in the Empire State! Red wine is symbolic of the blood ingested by the Reptilians. The wine can become sanctified as it did in the Roman Catholic Church, a patsy for the Reptilians. In the Catholic Church, wine replaced the blood in ceremony.

The Illuminati here on Earth have established a pyramid structure of control identical to the system that exists in the Draco Empire. The pyramid with the Reptilian eye, located on the American one-dollar bill, is symbolic of this control structure. The eye is the cap on the pyramid, thus explaining why the original surface of the Great Pyramid in Egypt was capped in solid gold.

The Pindar is represented by the gold cap on the pyramid. The next layer, or "eye," on the pyramid represents the 13 ruling families. They are as follows:

1. Rothschild (Bauer or Bower[1]) – Pindar
2. Bruce
3. Cavendish (Kennedy)
4. De Medici
5. Hanover
6. Hapsburg
7. Krupp
8. Plantagenet
9. Rockefeller
10. Romanov
11. Sinclair (St. Clair)
12. Warburg (del Banco)
13. Windsor (Saxe-Coburg-Gothe)

Each of the 13 ruling families is given an area of the Earth and/or a particular function to fulfill on the Earth. These particular functions include global finances, military technology/development, mind-control, religion, and media.

Each of the 13 ruling families has a council of 13 as well. The number, 13, has great significance to them. They know that there are 12 types of energies that pass through the 10 aspects of God-Mind. The totality of the 12 energies equals a 13th energy. This is considered the most powerful knowledge.

They also know that there are really 13 Zodiac signs, not the commonly acknowledged 12. They have kept the 13th hidden for centuries because it is the sign of the Dragon. They keep the qualities and traits of this sign secret to avoid giving away clues to the Reptilian mind-pattern.

The next layer is the second-in-command families who do the support work for the Pindar and 13 ruling families. While all of the 13 ruling family members are shapeshifters, all members of the 300 supporting families are not. They do, however, all have a high percentage of Reptilian DNA.

They are known as the "Committee of 300." These families include such notable names as Agnelli, Balliol, Beale, Bell, Bouvier, Bush, Cameron, Campbell, Carnegie, Carrington, Coolidge, Delano, Douglas, Ford, Gardner, Graham, Hamilton, Harriman, Heinz, Kuhn, Lindsay, Loeb, Mellon, Montgomery, Morgan, Norman, Oppenheimer, Rhodes, Roosevelt, Russell, Savoy, Schiff, Seton, Spencer, Stewart/Stuart, Taft, and Wilson. There are many others.

The Committee of 300 use many well-known institutions to accomplish their goals, including the Council on Foreign Relations, Bilderburgers, Trilateral Commission, Club of Rome, Royal Institute for International Affairs, Mafia, CIA, NSA, Mossad, Secret Service, International Monetary Fund, Federal Reserve, Internal Revenue Service, and Interpol, to name a few. All of these are private organizations or corporations set up as public service devices, but this is far from the truth.

The Illuminati structure also creates artificial countries to further their goals. Examples of these are the United States, Switzerland, Kuwait, the Soviet Union, Panama, Israel, Italy, Yugoslavia, the United Kingdom, most of Black Africa, all of the Arab countries, and all of Central and South America. These nations were created to amass wealth for the ruling families and their supporters, to hide or keep their wealth, and to create unstable conditions necessary to start wars or increase military budgets.

Switzerland was created as a neutral banking center so that Illuminati families would have a safe place to keep their funds without fear of destruction from wars and prying eyes.

The United States was established with 13 colonies, one for each of the Illuminati families. The original flag had 13 stars, and still has 13 stripes. The eagle, the symbol of the United States, holds 13 arrows in its talons. The United States is actually a corporate asset of the Virginia Company that was established in 1604 in England with direct involvement of the Rothschilds. The finances of the Rothschilds were necessary to fund the exploration and exploitation of the North American continent.

The assets of the Virginia Company, including the United States, are owned by the Holy Roman Empire via the Vatican. This occurred in 1213 when King James gave all English assets to the Reptilian Pope. Executorship remains with the British royal family, but actual ownership lies with the Roman Catholic Church.

The United States of America is not named after Amerigo Vespucci, as you learned in school. The Illuminati would never name a continent, actually two continents, after an Italian mapmaker. The name is actually a combination of words. "Am" is the Hebrew word for "people." "Ame" is also the command form of the Spanish/Latin verb "to love." "Eri" or "ari" is a Hebrew term for "lion." "Rica" is the feminine form of the Spanish word for "rich." "Ka" is the ancient Egyptian word for soul, or spirit force within a body.

There are two layers of meanings. The Ancient Hebrew/Egyptian translates to say, " the people of the lion with spirit force." Hence, the pyramid and all-seeing eye on the one-dollar bill. The Latinized version translates to say, "love riches," in a feminized/physical reality way. This gives an idea of what they had in mind.

Take this a step further, and one sees the mixture of the feminine Latin/eagle ideas with the masculine Hebrew/lion ideas. The symbolic statement of America is that it is a combination of Lemuria and Atlantis; a blend of the human/Lyrae with Reptilian/Draco. Perhaps the anagram LSD, an Illuminati created drug, has a hidden meaning as well:

Lyrae-Sirius-Draco! The combination of these three civilizations would produce the most powerful, technological Empire ever known!

In 1776, the creation of the United States as an independent nation coincided with the declaration into public existence of the official Illuminati organization by member Adam Weishaupt, in Bavaria. Publicly, Mr. Weishaupt appeared to be determined to create an organization comprised of the European elite that would uplift mankind.

Of course, this was part of an Illuminati global ceremony. The creation of the United States and the Illuminati organization were artificial beginnings for public consumption. The United States was the device to be used to bring the Illuminati into public acceptance. Current Illuminati members believe that Adam Weishaupt was a lookalike for George Washington, and it is actually Weishaupt's image that appears on the one dollar bill.

George Washington was a wealthy slave and plantation owner. He is known to have raped some of his female slaves and used some of the male slaves in ritualistic ceremony. There are many people of the Black race who can literally trace their genetics to the founding fathers. George Washington also ordered the building of the Montauk Lighthouse in 1796. This lighthouse included an underground area for supply storage in case of a Bristish coastline invasion. If he had only known what that area would become - or did he?

The 13 ruling Illuminati families constantly vie for control amongst themselves. During this time period, the Spanish, British, and French Illuminati all fought to win control over North and South America. The Rothschilds kept these Illuminati factions in line by sending Hessian troops to monitor the situation. The leaders enjoyed these war games, pitting one against the other to see who would win. The hundreds of thousands of lives lost were meaningless to them.

The Manifest Destiny of the United States was created to expand the territory of the Aryans at the expense of the native populations. As always, the Illuminati seek to destroy native peoples and their cultures. This is an attempt to destroy their knowledge of God-Mind, as well as the possibility that the natives will impart this information on to others.

Especially important is their need to eliminate native cultures with ancient knowledge of Atlantis and Lyrae.

The natives that gave them the most problem were the Cherokee Indians because this tribe retained most of their Atlantean knowledge, even accessing the Bear/Bigfoot frequency for information. For this reason, these people were uprooted from their homeland in the southern Appalachian Mountains, and forcibly marched to Oklahoma on what is now known as "The Trail of Tears." Many died along the way. Only a remnant remained in North Carolina, Tennessee, and Georgia. In the north, the vast Iroquois/Mohawk nation was disbanded. The Montauk, direct descendents of the Atlanteans who call their leader Pharaoh, were systematically eliminated.

The Rothschilds were aggressively involved with the slave trade from Africa, importing slaves to North and South America as well as the Caribbean. They were very careful not to import Blacks from the eastern areas of Ethiopia or Sudan where the descendents of Solomon were located, instead concentrating on western and central Africa for the slave populations. These areas had the pure mixture of Annunnakki and simian genetics, and the programming desirable for the Illuminati agenda.

The Rothschilds decided that splitting the United States colonies would double their profits. So they politically created, and financially supported, the Civil War. The Civil War was actually a global ceremonial ritual to bring slavery to its next level. This war allowed the North to "win," and publicly abolish slavery. The best slaves are the ones who do not realize that they are slaves. This alleviates rebellion and resistance. This was the status immediately following the Civil War. Blacks in the South are still slaves. There is still segregation, even in the North. The Illuminati still consider Blacks to be second or third class citizens. Only now the slavery is subtle and masked.

Since the Civil War, there have been other staged wars that entrenched the trend toward globalization. The Spanish-American War of 1898-1899 acquired more land for the American Illuminati, placing a greater portion of the Earth's surface under American jurisdiction. World War I was designed to change the map of Europe as well as test germ and chemical warfare technology for future use. This coincided with the worldwide influenza outbreak designed to reduce the global population, making control easier. World War I also laid the foundation for the German role in the next war.

World War II was a test of the final globalization and extermination projects. It was also designed to test mind-control machinations; to test the use of fluoride which deadens brain activity and slows resistance to authority; to experiment with slave labor camps and study the development of resistance; and to teach the masses to spy and report on one another.

World War II brought three primary goals of the Illuminati to fruition. The first was that hidden Illuminati symbolisms were brought to public attention from the underground strongholds in Tibet and Egypt, such as the Swastika and the ankh. The second was the creation of the State of Israel as a foundation for the New World Religion. The last was the creation of nuclear weapons as part of the Illuminati global ceremony.

During World War II, the Germans helped to perfect "sex-slaves" as a means of transmitting information amongst the elite. Sex-slaves can be either male or female, who are sexually programmed using Wilhelm Reich procedures, which are illegal in the United States, but used by the Illuminati and government.

These sex-slaves deliver messages and keep programmed sleepers in line. The sex-slave is downloaded with a message or function through various sexual acts and drugs, which can only be released by repeating the same sexual act with the target, or person, to be activated. They are trained to know their target's trigger words and trigger events to activate, delete, or change programming.

In recent years, several women have come forward claiming to be the sex-slaves of globally recognized political figures. Many were used as information couriers between high-level male Illuminati. Usually, lookalikes of the political figures are used in the incipient programming as a focal point for the sex-slave. The slave is put through a desensitizing process, so there is no pleasure in the sexual act; it is merely a duty to be performed. Many times the slave becomes sexually promiscuous, repeatedly having sex with people who look like the intended target. It is a sad life.

By the end of World War II, one of the three major Illuminati global rituals was accomplished. This was the nuclear explosion that took place in 1945 at the 33rd parallel as a test for the nuclear attack on Japan. This explosion was symbolic, representing the simultaneous creation and destruction of matter and energy. The year was symbolic as well. In numerology, $1 + 9 = 10$, representing the 10 aspects of God-Mind. The number 10 further breaks down to $1 + 0 = 1$, representing a new beginning. Continuing, $4 + 5 = 9$, representing the end of a cycle. Symbolically, the entire event represented the end of a cycle to prepare for a new beginning using the new creation of God-Mind out of destruction.

Additionally, a cylinder containing material still not explained by the government was trucked into the nuclear explosion testing. This cylinder was made from pure steel and allegedly was the same physical dimensions as the Kabala describes for the creation of Golems. Kabala is ancient Hebrew metaphysics that has been a staple for the Illuminati for millennia. Golems are artificial beings that are used as a slave force. It is highly probable that this was a symbolic ritual for the creation of a society of Golems.

World War II also allowed the European/American Illuminati to destroy the Japanese Illuminati desires of global domination. The Japanese royal family, represented by Emperor Hirohito, have always been ostracized as non-legitimate by the ruling 13 families. The Japanese claim to be direct descendents of Lemurian purebred Reptilians.

The European/American Illuminati claim that the Japanese Illuminati are descendents from a lower species in the Draco hierarchy. This lower species is considered a worker class without any political clout or influence. The European/American Illuminati also claim that East Indians are a lower species in the Draco hierarchy. The 13 ruling families consider light skin and hair to be an elite characteristic.

On January 17, 1994, Japan sent a seismic event to California. Exactly one year later on January 17, 1995, the city of Kobe, Japan was seismically destroyed. Kobe was the home of the Japanese electromagnetic weaponry centers. The European/American Illuminati will not tolerate thorns in their sides. The destruction of Japan and its royal family will continue in the coming months.

Every year, the Illuminati hold meetings to plan the events of the coming year to accomplish their main objective formulated millennia ago of global control and domination. In the 1850s, they pinpointed their target date for complete domination with an agenda called Plan 2000. This has since been revised to 2003. The fiasco election of George W. Bush Jr. to office is a key sign that they are on target. The public lesson of the United States presidential "election" of 2000 is that the citizens *do not* vote for anyone! Even the Illuminati are now finding it increasingly difficult to conceal their plans.

---

[1] The names in brackets are the original names, or a related name.

16

BLOOD-RITUAL & CEREMONY

There are many different kinds of ritual and ceremony that are performed as part of the Reptilian belief structure. It is not pleasant to read about, let alone witness. However, it is important to be informed, especially because these rites involve global leadership figures that control every aspect of daily life.

The most common ceremony performed by the hybrids is the ingestion of human blood and hormones to maintain the human form. Without these substances, the Reptilian mind-pattern would activate their DNA and they would look like lizards.

Depending on the need of the individual, this might be necessary as often as every few days, or perhaps only every few months. Two key factors are the age of the individual, and the percentage of Reptilian/human DNA. Older hybrids as well as those with more Reptilian genetics need the human harmonics more often.

The primary way to receive this energy is through blood. Human semen is considered the most potent booster because it contains hormones, genetic material, and blood. An all-in-one tonic, if you will.

The procedure can be as simple as fellatio. Or, it can be more complicated like bloodletting and actual eating of internal organs and/or genitalia. The latter implies death by murder. Many missing children and young adults meet their end this way. The hybrids particularly like the young, as their blood and hormones are more energetic. Menstruating women are also considered a prize since blood from the womb is considered highly potent, as are the hormones of pregnant women.

When produced during heightened sexual activity, these fluids are particularly strong, therefore enhancing the human energy of the hybrids for a more prolonged period of time. The death of the supplier is not necessary for this particular type of exchange. But, if the supplier is an unwilling participant, death may be necessary to keep the event a secret.

There are areas on and in the Earth where people are kept for the sole purpose of hormone production. These are primarily women kept for breeding to provide the necessary biological substances.

Often the blood or body fluid is mixed with an accelerant such as red wine, arsenic, herbs, or milk to increase the biological energy even further. Pornography is promoted worldwide to activate sexual desires and activities, making it easier to find willing ceremony participants. Drugs and sexual activity both enhance Illuminati ritual energy.

Another type of ceremony involves sexual magic. This ritual is designed to use the energy produced during heightened orgasmic activation to physically manifest a specific event or object. In other words, whatever thought is released into the ethers at the moment of intense orgasm is then propelled into existence. This is what is meant by the Illuminati when they rewrote the Bible and said, "whenever two or more are gathered in my name."

When two or more people simultaneously engage in intense sexual activity, the energy to manifest the goal of the event is multiplied. This is why group sex and orgies have been promoted for centuries. Because male body energy is more powerful than the feminine body energy, the Illuminati prefer a minimum of two males performing with a single female because of the semen. Symbolically, this represents the finite physical reality and the infinite non-physical. Currently, the drug known as ecstasy, which increases libido, and the so-called "date rape" drugs are the latest catalysts to enhance sexual magic activity.

Because the Reptilians are inherently androgynous, it is unimportant whether sex is with a male or female. To them, it is all the same. They prefer males because of the powerful energy boost from the male body. Female energy tends to draw into itself, and therefore is more desirable for sexual magic. The female represents physical reality, or Mother Earth, accepting the powerful male, non-physical, Father Sun energy, to create something on the planet. This explains the symbolism. For these reasons, bisexuality is the promoted lifestyle in the New World Order.

The next major ceremony performed is the "Religious Rite." This Reptilian religious service is performed on specific days or nights of the year, as an attempt to invoke astral level entities or demons for the purpose of fulfilling Illuminati control agendas. These rituals take several forms, including ritualistic killings, bloodletting, sexual rites, hunting and sacrificing, and even demonic manifestations.

These events usually occur on specific energy centers of the Earth where the energy produced can easily enter into the morphogenetic grid, and replicate everywhere. As an analogy, the morphogenetic grid is similar to the Earth's chakra system and DNA. This grid amplifies and reproduces the energetic effect like a hologram at all other points on the grid.

Major energy centers on the Earth used for these ceremonies include Land's End and Loch Ness in the United Kingdom, Rennes-Le-Chateau and Brittany in France, Bavaria in Germany, Montauk Point, Russian River, the Mojave Desert, the Channel Islands, Phoenix, and the east coast of Florida in the United States.

Any area on the 33rd and 42nd parallels in the Northern and Southern Hemispheres are used, as well as any area where there is a major crossing of Ley lines. Common places for ceremony include the Great Pyramid in Egypt, and in the great castles of Europe that are located over underground entrances to the inner Earth. These openings are most commonly found in Scotland, France, and Switzerland, with others in Belgium, Germany, and Austria.

A typical Religious Rite ceremony attended by most of the world leaders and corporate elite of the planet usually begins at dawn. Several "animals" are released into a protected wilderness area. These are humans chosen for their strength and power. They are usually male, but may include females, and can be of any race. The "animals" are usually drugged with amphetamines to make the "hunt" more interesting. These hunters are armed with guns, knives, and sometimes bows and arrows.

The prey is usually allowed to run and wander until dusk. The area is booby-trapped to the advantage of the mostly intoxicated hunters. During the course of the day, some prey is caught in the traps. They are tortured, raped, and killed by the hunters. Their bodies are burned. Sometimes parts of the bodies are kept as trophies.

At dusk, the remainder of the prey are rounded up and secured. The non-white victims are killed on the spot. There is usually a great bonfire before a Reptilian statue or idol, such as Nimrod, Osirus, or Belial, to whom the souls of these victims are dedicated. The ashes and bones of these sacrifices are kept in a pit in front of the idol. Their eyes, hearts, and sexual organs are often removed and fed to lizards and other vicious pets kept at the site. The "congregation" is plied with red wine and vodka, representing blood and hormones of the victims. Sometimes this is mixed with the ashes of the victims and buttermilk, representing semen.

The white/Aryan prey are drugged and taken to a staging area for the ritual. Depending upon the location, this could be outdoors in front of an altar, or in the depths of a castle, church, or political building.

After dusk there is a huge banquet that lasts for hours. Often the participants are dressed in a period costume. This might be Roman togas,

Victorian formal wear, Egyptian cloaks, or even Medieval armor. The costume depends on the holiday and the ceremony date of origin. These events occur on the Spring and Autumn Equinoxes, winter and summer solstices, All Hallow's Eve, Christmas Day — which is really the Roman Feast of Saturnalia, New Year's Day, Valentine's Day, the Ides of March, any Friday the 13th, and on Guy Fawke's Day, which is also my birthday, on November 5th. These days have entirely different significances to the Reptilians than they do to the general public.

At the banquet feast, there sometimes are place settings on the table before completely empty chairs. Servants bring food to these places, and the food actually disappears, even though no one can be seen sitting there! These are astral beings or non-physical Reptilians who are able to manifest energy in physical realms to participate in the event.

After dinner, the participants usually make a toast to specific past accomplishments and future events. Participants then exchange their costumes for robes of various colors. These are predominantly red, but some are black, some deep blue, and some bright yellow or gold, depending on their status in the ceremony.

Next, they retire to the ceremony chamber or outdoor area, depending upon weather and location. These ceremony locations are lit only by fire, including torches, candles, open pits, and wall sconces. The altar is either at the center of the room or open area, or against a stone wall raised on a platform. Tied down to the stone or golden altar is the main focus of the ceremony. In my experience, this has always been a male. He is called the "Vessel" or "Grail."

The ritual is presided over by two figures - a female, called the Mother Goddess, and a male, called the Father God. The Goddess is dressed in Red and Gold, and the God in White and Gold. They have hooded assistants dressed in black. These two ritual leaders are highly trained in psychic arts and mental manipulation. They use words to trigger the participants into a frenzy.

The most successful hunter comes in with the nude, white captured prey from earlier in the day. This hunter is called the Presenter. He ties the hands and feet of the victims and hoists them above the crowd by straps of leather under their chins. Inside, this is done with specially constructed copper poles. Outside, tree limbs are used which have copper strips wrapped around them. The crowd gathers underneath the victims, removing their robes.

As the crowd chants, they poke at the hanging victims with pitchforks, knives, and swords. They work to evoke fear and anxiety with small wounds until the victim is so terrified that a final thrust of a blade disembowels the victim, resulting in rivers of blood flowing over the crowd's bodies. The frenzy at this point is so high, that many begin to shapeshift into their Reptilian forms. Many even attack each other mindlessly.

Next, the crowd literally tears apart the hanging bodies, consuming the internal organs and genitalia. Many mix the dripping blood with red wine, vodka, and sometimes even arsenic, and drink it. In North America and western Europe, red wine is used along with a mixture of blood, arsenic, and hormonal fluids. This is a standard tonic during the middle and end of the rituals. In Asia, especially Central Asia and India, they add cinnamon to make a paste of the semen and menstrual blood for ingestion. In Eastern Europe they always add vodka and caviar to the drink of red wine and blood. In all places they often float the testicles and ovaries of sacrificial victims in the tonics.

Next, the God and Goddess then chant ceremonial invocation to the astral planes. I have heard this chant in Latin, Hebrew, Ancient Egyptian, Sumerian, German, English, and a guttural, hissing language which I was told is the original Draco language. The crowd repeats many of the verses chanted by the two leaders.

The two leaders both sexually stimulate the male tied onto the altar until he has an erection. Then, clamps are placed on the male's nipples, base of the penis, and scrotum. His legs are spread apart. His body is oiled with crocodile fat and small cuts are made over the main chakra areas, forming trickles of blood. The male is stood up, but still restrained. His arms are tied to a pole above him, his legs spread and tied to stones on the floor.

The God and Goddess open their robes and sexually stimulate each other while chanting. The Vessel, still sexually stimulated becomes "possessed" by the astral entity being invoked by the God and Goddess. The Goddess is then carried by the God with his erection inside of her. He circles the Vessel. Sometimes the Goddess is carried face forward, sometimes she faces the God as he carries her, and sometimes they are in a standing "69" position. All of this depends on the entity being manifested.

The Vessel may assume strange characteristics as he becomes "occupied" by the entity. Sometimes he speaks in a different language. Sometimes he gives a command and the crowd chants. The Vessel is considered to be as "holy" as the God and Goddess in the ceremony. There are only a handful of Gods and Goddesses in the world, but several Vessels. They are reused due to their abilities to host the entity. If they fail, they are executed.

At the height of the ceremony, the God signals the crowd to approach the Vessel. They touch him, licking the blood and genitalia in an effort to absorb the energy of the entity.

They drink the Vessel's sweat and try to squeeze the penis for a drop of fluid. Oral and anal intercourse is allowed with the Vessel to merge their energy with the entity. Anal intercourse is also used as a symbolic gesture of submission, and can be used as an internal programming activator. Oral intercourse is used as both a status determinant and an energetic booster.

When the participants are done with this, the Vessel is placed back on the altar. The God and Goddess disengage from one another and the Goddess orally ejaculates the Vessel, swallowing the semen. At the same time, the God places his erection in the mouth of the Vessel as a symbol of domination and control. After this, the God and the Goddess stand on the altar over the Vessel and the God enters his erection into the Goddess from the rear and ejaculates, culminating the ceremony. Rubbing semen all over the body is considered to be a powerful rejuvenator, by both males and females.

At this point, all of the participants merge into an orgiastic fest that lasts until dawn. The God, Goddess, and Vessel leave the premises after the God ejaculates. If the Goddess becomes pregnant during any of these ceremonies, either the fetus or the newborn infant is used in ritualistic sacrifice.

It is not uncommon for tattoos, skin carvings, and piercings to be found on the bodies of the God, Goddess, and Vessel. These are designed to hold the energy of the ceremony. The Goddess is almost always red-haired with green or blue eyes. She is thin and delicate with very white skin. The God is almost always muscular and tall, and is often of the Lion frequency. He has dark blonde to light brown hair, with green or blue eyes. If he also has Bear energy, his hair may be dark, but his eyes must be light.

The Vessel may graduate after a time to become a God. A breeder can graduate to become a Goddess. All three positions are heavily protected in the Illuminati culture. The semen of the Vessel and the God, known for its power, fertility, and activation, is a prized possession. Rubbing it on the body is said to open locked genetics and mind-patterns. People who spend a lot of time with these individuals find their life becoming emotionally volatile, and physical changes begin to occur.

Another type of ritual performed involves mind-control and manipulation. This was commonly practiced at the Montauk Project, but was also used in private matters among Illuminati. It was also used by the Soviets at the Filatov Institute in Odessa and at Tavistok in Britain.

Using this method, the subject, mostly male, is brought to the point of near orgasm, and then held there. When the body is in this state, the mind is completely open. Information, programming, and memory can be placed in the cells of the body or in the mind-pattern. The reverse is true also, where in this state the mind and cellular structure can be downloaded using Wilhelm Reich procedures.

Sometimes during programming sessions, a male would be made to ejaculate after biting the penis and drawing blood. Ingesting this combination of fluids at the point of orgasm, and while the male was in a state of fear, is considered a tremendous energy enhancer.

Generally, men are sent by the Illuminati to trigger or block female targets, and females are sent to male targets. The triggers are usually sexual, but can be stimulated by drugs and alcohol. The agents also use cigarettes to ground themselves when he/she is working. These agents also tend to have sugar cravings because their programming disrupts hormonal productions, such as insulin, and are prone to unstable blood sugar levels. Most of the agents are bisexual so that they can be used in any situation. Anyone interested in this type of ritual or sexual programming can find more information in the *Montauk Project* book series.

The most heinous type of ritual ceremony performed by the Illuminati is the serial killings, accompanied by global media coverage of the event, especially in the case of major figures. The term, serial killing, is related to the word, cereal, which in turn is derived from the Greek Goddess Ceres. Ceres was the Goddess who presided over grain harvests. Many sacrifices were offered to her for improved harvest yields. Much of the Illuminati ceremonial rites are derived from cultural habits from the past.

Over the years there have been many sacrificial killings to Ceres designed to create a crop of harvestable humans. One of the first globally reported serial killings was the Jack the Ripper case in London. These prostitutes were found with their internal organs removed with the surgical precision of a medical professional. The number one suspect is the royal physician, Sir William Gull. He was a Mason and Queen Victoria's personal doctor.

Other killings over the years that received global attention were the killings by Richard Speck in Chicago, Son of Sam in New York, Charles Manson in Los Angeles, Richard Dahmer in the Midwest, and the Unibomber. All of these murders have symbolisms not publicized by the investigators. All of them took place on or near the 33rd or 42nd parallels.

Masonic symbol information and books written about these murders reveal the undeniable Illuminati signatures

Other symbolic Illuminati ritual killings include the John F. Kennedy assassination, the murder of JonBenet Ramsey, the execution of Princess Diana, the shooting down of TWA 800, Swissair 101, Egyptair 990, John F. Kennedy, Jr., Alaska Airlines 283, and Pan Am 103. The locations, people killed, dates, and cover-ups all have ritualistic significance. These were no accidents. They were planned, staged, strategic sacrifices in a global blood ritual that altered human consciousness and mind-patterns.

Every year, literally millions of people disappear off the face of the Earth, never to be seen or heard from again. Many have legitimate accidents or are runaways. Most, are the victims of ceremonial ritualistic events as outlined above. Many of the small children whose faces appear on milk cartons are the victims of experiments similar to the Montauk and Monarch Projects. They fit the profile of young, fair-haired children with genetics perfect for mind-control work.

The Illuminati love symbolism, dates, name derivatives, and double meanings that cryptically tell the truth while hiding it from the general population. With the advances of media technology, and the ability to transmit subliminal and overt messages, the temptation to globalize their rituals and ceremonies has grown exponentially. The first attempt by the Illuminati in the 20th Century was the creation of a Santa Claus in a red suit. Previously, this figure was known as St. Nicholas and Father Christmas. Now, Santa is the enthrallment of children. The word "Santa" is an anagram for Satan.

Satanism and Satanic rituals have grown exponentially since the media blitz of the Red Santa. This subliminal method instills in the mind-pattern that a mystical, non-human can enter people's homes. He will be good to them *only* if they behave a certain way during the year. The red costume speaks for itself – red is the color code for entry into the astral planes. Red is the color code used by the Goddess during the Reptilian ritual to invoke astral entities.

Of course, Santa lives at the North Pole, which is an entry point into the inner Earth, and the underground Reptilian society. He has short little elves that do his work, symbolic of the small greys with a group mind-pattern. The flying reindeer and sled symbolize the interdimensional flying craft used to enter there. Children are advised to leave Santa a snack for his arrival, representing a sacrificial offering to a powerful god. In addition, the commercialism behind this artificial Christmas holiday is designed to extract any religious intentions as well as enrich an already wealthy global elite.

Other global transmissions designed to instill respect and non-violence toward Reptilians include programs teaching children that Reptilians are their friends. There are a vast number of such programs, with the Flintstones, Teenage Mutant Ninja Turtles, Barney, and Pokeman among the more well-known.

Even the infamous Teletubbies, brought direct from Babylon-don (London), is designed to subliminally program young children with its mindless babble. Each of the four androgynous Teletubbies wears an archetype symbol on its head. This is a DNA sentence that translates to "activation from space to create robots." The program also depicts a living baby surrounded by a radiating sunburst, a Reptilian religious symbol. The baby at the center of the sun indicates that this baby is a sacrifice to the Sun God.

The numerous Satanic worship cults in the US, Canada, and western Europe are fronts for the Illuminati screening system to identify citizens that would make unquestioning robotical soldiers. Perpetrators who perform the most heinous crimes against the human body and spirit without a thought are the ones recruited as henchmen/women for Illuminati service.

In low-income Black communities where drugs and murder are common, watchful eyes identify those gang members and drug dealers who are without morals or regard for anyone. These become the assassins and expendable couriers for the Illuminati agenda within the public sphere. There is even a group of Black women hired as assassins called the "Dark Angels." They travel internationally to eliminate selected targets.

Victims are often left headless and handless, indicating the victim was considered a non-person, as well as the superiority of the killers. Male victims may have their genitalia removed, the penis shoved in the victim's mouth, or an object placed in their rectum. This simultaneously symbolizes the submissiveness of the victim, as well as a warning to others.

Police departments and the FBI, as well as all intelligence agencies are completely controlled by the Illuminati and their hierarchy. Most of the time, key clues and symbols found at the murder scene are not publicly revealed.

Most police chiefs are Masons. The six-pointed star on the police badge originates in Ancient Israel in the time of King Solomon, and literally means "as above, so below."

While this is generally understood to represent spiritual values applied to the Earth, the Masonic interpretation is that the Illuminati will control the Earth as gods.

King Solomon was an Illuminati and belonged to an ancient Egyptian cult. He sent the Ark of the Covenant to Ethiopia with Queen Sheba to secret it away for future Illuminati plans. He combined his Hebrew genetics with the Queen, creating an ancestry mixture of Sirians/ Annunnakki/Lyraens. When the Queen left Israel, she was pregnant with Solomon's child. Her descendent, Emperor Haile Selase, called himself the "Lion of Judah." His official symbol was the lion.

There was a vast population of Black Jews in Ethiopia called the Falasha.

In the 1980s Israel instigated the separation of the province of Eritrea from Ethiopia because the Ark of the Covenant was located in Eritrea for safekeeping. Israel created this war between Ethiopia and Eritrea as a cover for the Israelis to remove the Ark back to Egypt. This was accomplished under the guise of ferrying food and supplies to the Eritreans.

Israel then orchestrated a peace between the warring factions by convincing Ethiopia to release the Falasha to Israel. The Israelis did this because they did not want members of their genetic heritage to fall victim to the same fate intended for other Black Africans, i.e., the Illuminati death campaign to eliminate the Black race from the Earth using AIDS, Ebola, war, and starvation.

The AIDS virus was ritually released. First, the AIDS virus was tested on a terminally ill patient in St. Louis, Missouri. Then Martin Luther King, Jr. was assassinated in 1968. The last name of the alleged assassin, James Earl Ray, is a synonym for rey. In Spanish, "rey" translates into "king." To the Illuminati, the White King killed the Black King, assuring them of victory. After the Black King was killed, they released the virus into Africa and Haiti to complete the ritual.

Next, the Israelis will remove the Palestinians from Jerusalem and elsewhere in Israel, restore the Holy Temple to the Temple Mount, now occupied by the Dome of the Rock.

All of these ritualistic activities are examples of the twisted activities at Montauk and other military installations as well as castles, churches, private mansions, caves, tunnels, government buildings, and energy centers all over the Earth.

17

RITUAL IN RED

In the early to mid 1970s, I was performing the part of the Vessel. This was partly due to my lifetime as Johannes von Gruber.[1] The Johannes personality was of great importance to them. Although a high-ranking member of the Nazi party in Germany during the war, he entered into this timeline from an alternate reality. He was from a parallel universe where Nazi-like Reptilians had already taken over the entire galaxy and beyond. Apparently, they had put a lot of effort, time, and money in me. They were literally going to get the very last drop out of me.

Besides the Johannes personality, I was also desired for a Vessel because of my genetics. Within me is Lyraen (Aldebaran), Sirian (Hebrew), and Draco (Reptilian), with some added mixtures of Tau Ceti (Russian) and dolphin frequency. This means that I have within me the genetics of both the Lion and Bear. On one occasion, I was shown that scorpion genetic material is also part of my composition. Such a combination is rare even in genetic experiments. This is why my semen was so valuable to the Illuminati, and explains why I was allowed to be the Vessel at a relatively young age. I was "promoted" to the title of Father God for purposes of the rituals.

I have many non-compatible strains of DNA within me, as well as three separate soul-personalities, all using one body. It was no wonder that I was made to exercise constantly and build up my physical girth. By the time I was 30, my body was extremely powerful and muscular. My physical strength was incredible. It was the only way to contain all of this genetic structure within me, in physical reality.

I have many memories of Illuminati ceremonies from my 13 years at Montuak. Besides the "normal" daily programming and experimentation, these ceremonies were held several times a year, including Valentine's Day, both equinoxes, both solstices, and Halloween.

I was three or four years old when I was first brought to these rituals two or three times a year. There were some years when nothing like this happened. Voices played over and over in my head, telling me never to tell anyone or I would get sick and die. These voices threatened my parents, even playing scenes in my mind of their destruction.

During the ceremonies, I remember looking up to see the Goddess standing over me in a deep red, hooded robe. I could see the flash of her green eyes and the shock of her long red hair peeking out from under the robe. I was always drugged into an induced state of higher consciousness. I was only vaguely aware of my body, but I knew that I was totally nude, and strapped down to a hard and uncomfortable table. It felt like smooth stone or wood. I was not certain.

The room was always dimly lit. I could make out torches held by sconces on the wall behind the Goddess. She was frighteningly beautiful and her presence excited me to a sexual frenzy. Although I could not completely feel my body, I was aware of a huge erection and a pulsating sensation in my groin. She stood above me with a sharp dagger held in both hands pointed over my heart area. I went through this many times. I knew that she would not kill me, but at the same time, I was never totally sure.

I was not able to move my head, even though there was nothing holding it down. Only my legs were clamped to this table, spread apart. My hands were fixed securely over my head, palms up, and together. My body felt cold, even though the room or chamber was always warm. I felt the perspiration on my forehead.

In the background, I always heard deep, almost inhuman voices saying something in another language that I mentally understood, but had no conscious memory of ever learning. This language was guttural and slow, and sounded like a record being played at the wrong speed underwater.

The Goddess always chanted in a low voice that I could barely hear. Her eyes were rolled up facing the ceiling. She appeared not in control of herself. It was scary and sexually exciting at the same time.

The ceiling was a grey blur, but the walls often looked like grey stones. My arms ached from remaining in the same position for so long. My legs went numb. My penis hurt from being erect and hard. I perceived uncomfortable clamps or vices on my nipples, scrotum, and the base of my penis. They were starting to become uncomfortable.

Hands with rough skin touched my body. I could not see anyone except the Goddess. My eyes were fixated on her alone. I felt myself ejaculating into a warm object that fit snuggly over the head of my penis.

I could feel a hand moving from the base of my penis, squeezing up the shaft, getting every last drop.

Next, the Goddess slowly moved the dagger to the middle of my chest, pressing until I felt the blade enter the surface of my skin. As I got older, it pulled my chest hair and pinched a little. I could feel warm drops of blood roll down the sides of my chest. What felt like a warm, wet cloth was applied. I later realized that the movement of this cloth felt more like a dog lapping up water from a bowl.

Everything at this point went blurry and dreamlike. I could no longer focus on anything or anyone. I became nauseous and headachy, feeling extremely dizzy. I drifted into a deep state of non-physical awareness as a kind of escape from this experience. It was a "here we go again" type of feeling.

I was never fully aware of how these experiences began, but I always seemed to wake up in the middle of them at approximately the same time. They usually ended with my drifting off into another reality. There was always the smell of sour milk and perspiration combined with a dusty sensation in the air, and I sensed great simultaneous combinations of excitement and fear.

I would find myself waking up at home in my bed, nude and without covers. I always first looked at the clock, feeling extremely exhausted. When I moved, I could feel a pinching at the center of my chest. Closer examination revealed a pimple, or what I perceived to be a mosquito bite that lasted for several days before disappearing.

I would have no memory of the incident upon waking, but after a couple of hours of activity, flashes of what I believed to be a dream would come to the forefront of my mind, leaving me with a feeling of importance or even superiority for some reason. I dreaded sleep, but would always perform the same bedtime ritual of concentration at the pineal gland. Then, I waited for something else to take over the effort. As a result of all my training and programming, my pineal gland is extremely active and enlarged.

The first urine of the morning was always painful after these episodes. I felt soreness in my back, arms, legs, and scrotum. My nipples would be so sensitive, that any clothing I wore irritated them. The hair around my ankles would thin, then completely fall out.

I also had irritation around my navel, and in my armpits. These symptoms lasted a couple of days before disappearing.

I became fascinated during my early life with robed figures and chanting. Blood made me cringe, and still does. I have an aversion to clamps and hard floors, preferring soft carpeting and uplifting music. I was taught that ejaculation was only for procreative purposes and should never be wasted, and that masturbation was wrong and useless.

Whenever I watched movies or television programs showing people tied up, tortured, or a weird ritual or ceremony taking place, I became excited and afraid at the same time.

I had no one to talk to about these experiences. I knew if I did, these experiences would be dismissed as hallucinations, nightmares, or drug-induced experiences. I knew that they were none of these. I had physical remnants on my body to prove that they actually occurred. These events began happening when I was a small child. I never knew or heard of such things in my daily life.

Thin, red-haired women with light eyes became my ideal. I always compared the women that I met to my ideal. If I dated a woman with any other color hair, I soon convinced her to either dye or highlight her hair red.

In the Marriage Program[2] at Montauk, the controllers attempted to mate specific females with specific males for breeding purposes. We could only have monitored sex with the one chosen for us.

Males were programmed to have erection and breathing problems if they desired sex with "outsiders." Females were programmed to only desire others during their menstrual cycles. This prevented unwanted pregnancies and of course, made it less likely that they would engage in any unauthorized sexual activity.

My first sexual encounter took place at the Montauk Air Force Base in 1970, when I was 14 years old. I was told that I was only allowed to have relations with women that were chosen for me because of the nature of the genetic experimentation. In addition, I was told that I was genetically created for specific purposes and could not mix my "blend" with just anyone.

Shortly after moving to Long Island during the summer of 1970, I was at the base when I was suddenly brought to a room that appeared very clinical. There was a full wall mirror on three sides, and a bolted door on the fourth wall. This room was completely white with linoleum flooring. Harsh florescent ceiling fixtures were mounted directly over a raised, soft-padded platform.

Here, I was stripped and immediately injected in the buttocks, making my knees go limp. I was grabbed before dropping to the floor, then laid out on a platform. Something that tasted like mouthwash and medicine was sprayed into my mouth. After what seemed like a long time, the bolted door opened. A young red-haired girl was practically dragged into the room by an older woman and a middle-aged man both dressed in a white medical coat. The girl was in a thin white robe, but it was open, exposing her thin, naked body. I had never seen red pubic hair before. I found it strange-looking, but exciting.

They draped the girl on the platform next to me, removing her robe. They sprayed something in her mouth, too. She was so thin that I could see every rib and bone in her body. The two people in the white coats left the room.

By now, I was wide awake, but still felt like I had taken some kind of mind-altering drug. The room was blurry and actually felt warm. I immediately noticed that I had a tremendous erection. I felt my heart racing, and an extremely aggressive side of me began to emerge.

I really did not know what I was doing, and although I felt like I was doing the wrong thing, I began to sexually touch this pretty red-haired girl. With every touch, she favorably responded, even though she was not fully conscious. Her eyes were only half open, sometimes appearing to be completely shut. I continued until I reached full orgasm inside of her. She did not look much older than me, but she appeared to be more physically mature. I do not know how she felt about the experience, but I do not really believe that she even knew what had happened.

When I withdrew from her, I studied her essence completely. I felt like a baby chick emerging from an eggshell that identifies the first thing that it sees as its mother. Well, from that time forward, this red-haired girl/woman became my ideal for sex. As I studied her, I noticed that my erection was still there. I believe I heard a female voice over the intercom. I do not know what it said, but all I know is that I was inside her again. The second orgasm was more intense than the first, actually hurting me.

Before I could dismount, I felt cold, strong hands grabbing my arms, pulling me away. Everything went blurry, although I recall people entering the room and talking. When I awoke, I was in a medical unit dressed in pajamas, covered up to my chest. When I tried to lift my head, I felt severe pain like a blinding migraine. So, I continued to lie down.

Two or three people eventually stood by my bed. One held my right arm and spoke to me. I was told that this girl I had been with was tested for compatibility with my energy field. Although she was genetically appropriate, there was not a good match. A second voice said that another, more suitable "mate" would be chosen for me. They also told me that I was tested for my sexual capabilities. Since I did so well, they would implant a device behind my scrotum to increase my fertility and regulate my sexual activity.

Next thing I knew, I was wheeled on a gurney into another room with bright lights and tied to some type of operating table. I was completely nude again, and injected in the groin, arm, and buttocks. I passed out.

I awoke at home, in my own bed. I had an irritation in my groin and big mosquito bite on my arm and buttocks. When I urinated, it burned. My testicles hurt. Many years later I found a lump behind my left testicle which was diagnosed as a varicocele. It was supposed to make me less fertile, so the doctor said. Tell that to my seven children!

This implant actually enhances my sperm production. My semen is extremely fertile, and was frequently taken and used. Because of this trait, I was sent all over the world at various times of the year to perform my role as Vessel. The ritual components did not vary much in the different locales, however, the nuances varied depending upon the development of the indigenous Reptilian hybrid subcultures.

During my time as a Vessel in Montauk, many well-known personalities came to participate. Some of these were political figures, while others were in the media or literary world. I remember seeing personages that looked like Sir Laurence Gardner, William F. Buckley, Sean Connery, Spiro Agnew, Henry Kissinger, John F. Kennedy, Jr., the Shah of Iran, and numerous other actors, military personnel, and Middle Eastern figures whose names I did not know. All but Kennedy and Connery shapeshifted into Reptilian form during the ceremonies.

On most occasions they gorge on fetuses harvested from abortion clinics. They also had live babies that they held up by the back of the neck. Then, they slashed its throat from left to right, ear to ear, biting down on the gapping opening to drink the blood. This was an amazing delicacy to them.

I was told many things at Montauk, such as how the lower levels held women in cages who were raped or inseminated, and the resulting fetuses and babies used in rituals, or simply whenever needed by the hybrids to maintain human form.

They told me how in Viet Nam, parachuting airmen were often captured and slaughtered for their hormones by their own people who were working for the Reptilians. It is a known fact that sometimes the bodies of airmen were found in the jungle with the blood drained and all the soft tissues removed, including eyes, lips, anus, genitals, and nipples.

I was also told that the cattle mutilations that occurred in the western USA and elsewhere were performed by grey aliens needing hormones who could not get them from ritual or from their controllers. Many people do not realize that the greys are genetically created by the Reptilians to be drone workers and monitor humans. These greys are purposely created with hormonal deficiencies so that they remain dependent on their Reptilian masters. Some of these greys have become renegades, abducting humans and performing cattle mutilations in order to survive on their own. These renegades worked with pro-human factions of the N.W.O. but were being systematically poisoned by contaminated blood and hormones from abductees.

I assimilated all this information quite rapidly. I could download and understand information and instructions very quickly. This ability elevated my status from guinea pig to trainer in a matter of a few years. By the mid 1970s I was already preparing other children to work with the main psychic. I was used as a booster to the other psychics. I was sent on many missions. My training and programming at Montauk went smoothly from the perspective of my controllers. To me it was horrific.

I was simultaneously an experiment, a religious figure, a hormone producer, a breeder, a son, a brother, a father, an alien, and a human. I was provided with a personality alter for each of my roles. The key for my controllers was to keep the alters non-integrated. Triggers were used to activate each one. Most of the time, each alter was not consciously aware of the others. On deeper subconscious levels, they knew about each other.

[1&2] Refer to *Montauk: The Alien Connection (Sky Books, 1998)*.

18

MY LOST CHILDREN

In my previous books, I have written about my sons, Matthew, Jeremy, Daniel, and Zachary, and briefly about my daughter, Jaime. Since that time, Janet and I had another son, Jonathan, who was born in December 1998.

Jonathan's birth, and the events preceding it, was interesting. One year after Zachary was born, Janet became pregnant again. Because our insurance coverage had changed, we used a different obstetrician. This doctor was the head of the obstetrics department at SUNY/Stony Brook Hospital. She had an excellent reputation.

Janet was sick from the moment of conception, constantly vomiting and feeling ill. Her doctor said that these symptoms imply an abundance of pregnancy hormones, as well as a sign of a strong fetus and pregnancy.

Toward the end of the second month of her pregnancy when Janet went for an examination, the doctor told her that the heartbeat was strong. She said that Janet's uterus felt so large, that there was a high probability that she was carrying twins. She then ordered an immediate sonogram for Janet. The technician who performed the sonogram told Janet that something was not right, and wanted to take an internal sonogram.

While Janet prepared for this, a second doctor came in to help with the procedure. This time, they told her that they could not locate any heartbeat at all. Janet was told that the baby was dead, and that this happened in 25% of all pregnancies. Janet would need a D & C to remove it. We were both devastated. How could they hear a strong heartbeat, say it was possibly twins, then say it was dead, all within the scope of an hour or two?!

This reminded me of the incident with my last wife, when she had a three-month old ectopic pregnancy. At that time, the doctors refused to give us the lab report. My ex-wife also had a few pregnancies that vanished. Was this strangeness repeating itself again?

Several days later, Janet and I went to the hospital to have the doctor remove the fetus. Janet asked for one more sonogram to check for a heartbeat. She was told that there was none. The aftermath of this was emotionally very hard. Janet was completely depressed, and I became emotionally wild. We argued a lot and I was unkind. I could not stop myself. It felt like someone was pushing a button, and I turned on.

Soon after, we moved into our new house. It was a miracle that we even got the house, as it was a model home still being built when we first saw it. I passed by it several times without stopping, as it looked too expensive for us. One day, we stopped to ask the builder a question, and he told us that he needed to move the house and would drop the asking price $20,000! In addition, he gave us the appliances, carpeting, and ceiling fixtures, and allowed us to move in before the actual closing date. Anyone familiar with Long Island's housing market on Long Island in the late 90s knows that this is not a common practice.

This large home is on an acre and a quarter of land, and had just about everything we ever wanted for a price that was unreal. The situation was, again, similar to the experience I had with my ex-wife years before. In fact, the two houses are only a couple of miles apart. That is one of the main reason I wanted to live in the area—to live closer to my older children.

Within six months, Janet was pregnant again. This time things went smoothly. She called the doctor who performed the D & C and found out that shortly after our experience, she left the hospital. She was the head of the obstetrics department, and now she was gone! Strange indeed!

The doctor who delivered Zachary now took our insurance, so Janet returned to her. She had a scheduled caesarian. That morning we went into the hospital extremely early for the delivery preparations. Janet was taken into the operating room, while I changed into hospital scrubs. While I was in the well-lit hallway leaning down to put the covers over my sneakers, I glimpsed out of the corner of my eye to see a person coming toward me.

I looked up, and standing before me was a very tall, naked man. Now this was in a busy hospital in the daytime! Before I could straighten up or even speak, this man said, "Hello, I'm Jonathan." This was the name we had chosen for the new baby. Everything seemed surreal. I touched my eyes and body to make sure that I was awake.

The man continued, "When I am seventeen years old, I will do something that will make you excited." I responded, "When you are seventeen years old, I will be a very old daddy." He then said, "It's all in your mind anyway. I have to go now." With that, he turned toward the wall of the delivery room where Janet was being prepped, and walked right through the solid wall!

I straightened myself up and thought that maybe I had gotten up too early. I wondered about what he said. What kind of exciting thing would he do? Was it a "good" exciting, or a "bad" exciting? It seemed as though he was deliberately vague.

I was called into the delivery room because the surgery had already begun. I sat by Janet's head. There was a curtain by her neck preventing her from viewing the actual delivery. When they took Jonathan out of her womb, the first thing the nurse said was, "It's not a baby, it's a man!" My heart almost fell on the floor! How did they know what I just saw? I must have turned white because Janet was concerned about me. They cleaned him up and handed him to me. I held the baby and showed him to Janet while they closed her up. He was big and had man-like features. He did not look like a newborn. This was eerie to me considering what I just experienced.

Jonathan did not want to be a baby. When he was two weeks old and crying in his crib, I went in to give him a pacifier. He looked at me and swatted it out of my hand! I thought, "Oh, that was a lucky shot!" I tried again. He swatted it out of my hand a second time with determination and a look of disgust toward me. He was a man.

He cried like a Reptilian. His screeches were like those of a dinosaur, or at least I assumed it was. He had an anger in him and a temper. No one believed his real age. He held his head up five minutes after he was born He started walking at seven months. He opened up the child-proof locks on the cabinets before he was one. He was potty trained before the age of two. His intelligence is scary. He gives Zachary a run for his money. My older boys love him, too. I cannot wait to see what he does in 2015 when he turns seventeen!

During this time, I tried unsuccessfully to develop a relationship with Jaime. She was living in Connecticut with her mother. Mia was dating John Denver, and was devastated after his fatal plane crash. I believe that he committed suicide because he was despondent over his relationships and career. His small plane went up without enough fuel. He must have known that when he took off.

For Mia, this was the second boyfriend who died in a crash. She is not known for her stable relationships, and it looks like Jaime will follow in her mother's footsteps. I told her that she can always come to me if she is in trouble. I realize that she is angry at me for not being in her life when she was younger. She is rebelling with cigarettes, drinking, a tongue ring, and sexual promiscuity. She almost died as a result of an abortion. I know that one day she will mature. I will be waiting for her with open arms.

During this time, I was giving weekly classes on the Language of Hyperspace. I had many attendees, including Peter Moon, Preston Nichols, and Al Bielek. Duncan Cameron also came around from time to time. One evening, a Montauk boy showed up. He was working with Preston on deprogramming himself. His name was Morgan, like the pirate. Morgan had a French girlfriend who really loved him, although she was much older. She asked me to help train Morgan since he was not satisfied with the work he was doing with Preston. She was concerned about him. She said he related to me, and was fond of me. She said I was a father figure to him.

I remembered that I was told in prison that I had an older son with a child. I was told that I was going to find and train him. They told me that the boy's name was Armond, and that he was in Russia. The name, Morgan, contains all but one of the letters in Armond. I remembered the semen extraction that occurred in Miami in February 1973. Morgan was born in October of that year. His mother was a flight attendant for a major international airlines. Her husband was killed in a freak plane crash between Holland and Britain. They said the plane was hit by a tornado! Near Holland?

So, Morgan grew up without a father. He was a brilliant but extremely difficult child. His mother threw him out at the age of nine. He went to live with friends, and then in a home for challenged children. He lived a life of turmoil. He remembers being involved at the Montauk Project, and indeed, he lived in that area for a large part of his youth. He is the typical blonde with blue eyes.

Morgan and I had not discussed his past when he started coming to my house. He was living with an evil friend from New Mexico on the east end of Long Island. His daughter, Aria, lived with her mother in Montauk. One day, Morgan asked me about his heritage. He said he felt like his parents were not his parents, much as I did as a child. He wanted to know who his real father was. I gave him a mental DNA exercise to show him his true background. He called the next day and emotionally said that when he did the visualization, he saw me as his genetic father. The moment he said those words, I flashed back to Miami and the Cuban agents who took my semen to give to the Russians. I knew back then that a child would be the result, although I did not know how or where.

Since that day, Morgan has called me dad, and I have counted him amongst my children. After one of my classes, Morgan sat next to me, showing me some things he had drawn in his notes. An older man whom I had never met before stared at us while I spoke to Morgan. He then came up to us, and asked if we were related. He said he had never seen two people look so alike. Morgan and I just looked at each other and smiled. It is a good feeling when a third party, especially a stranger, confirms to you what you already know.

I have since introduced Morgan to some of his half-brothers, and told him about Jaime. Morgan feels an obligation to protect Jaime, and he does so in hyperspace. I taught Morgan much of what I know. He has some trouble with alcohol, and has been in a rehabilitation facility. He has difficulty relating to conventional society. This is a common theme amongst Montauk survivors. Morgan now lives with the mother of his new son, Ppayten, who he named based on the frequencies and codes outlined in my *The Healer's Handbook: A Journey Into Hyperspace (Sky Books, 1999)*. He lives on Long Island, and I visit as often as I can. Morgan is no longer lost to me. One day he will tell his own story.

19

AROUND THE WORLD

In the fall of 1998, I was invited to speak at the World UFO Congress in Zurich, Switzerland by a former Swiss filmmaker. I was thrilled to accept. While there I met Zachariah Sitchin, author of the Twelfth Planet book series, who turned out to be a disappointment. He was arrogant and self-centered. Even at breakfast he sat at a separate table. His wife and entourage ensured that no one approached him, and protected him from his soon-to-be not so adoring public.

I knew that I was there to teach and share my information, not maintain an air of superiority and distance. His lecture was also a disappointment, and the information appeared to be a reversal from his previous works. Perhaps he had been compromised or fulfilled his Illuminati commission. Now, he seemed to play games with the public.

I have observed that many of these congresses and expositions are filled with New Agers who promote peace, love, and light. They want to believe that the government is ignorant of the aliens desire to uplift mankind to a higher level. This attitude reminds me of an episode from television's *Twilight Zone* called, "To Serve Man." Aliens arriving on Earth give a book with that name to world leaders who in turn ask scientists to decipher it. Meanwhile, as the aliens take the humans on a "tour" of their homeworld, the scientists realize that "To Serve Man" is really a cookbook!

Such was the congress in Switzerland. However, they were receptive to me, except for my American humor. Because I see energy fields, they asked me what the auras of Swiss people look like. I responded that the only problem with Swiss auras were the many holes, in a humorous reference to their famous cheese. But, they took me seriously and asked what they could do about it. I found their response even more hilarious than my feeble attempt at comedy.

My Swiss sponsor invited me to return to Zurich for additional seminars. He suggested combining a seminar in Europe with a trip to Asia, concluding with a tour to a sacred crystal site in the Philippines, only visited once before by white people. It was an exciting proposition, but I would have to be gone for five weeks. After discussing the entire situation with Janet, who would be left alone with a baby and three-year old toddler, the arrangements were made.

At this point, I quit my full time job to have time to do my seminar work. My company was sorry to see me go because in the immigration work I did my error rate was less than 2 %. However, I found the work to be boring and the co-workers to be petty. I was grateful that I could finally leave this place.

Before leaving the states, I advertised the trip to visit the crystal in the Philippines, calling it the "Arcturus Experience." I planned to meet the Americans in Manila. One of the persons who signed up to go was a masculine woman whom I shall call "Devilla." She never used her real name, preferring to call herself by a color. I met her at a UFO Congress in Laughlin, Nevada earlier in the year.

Subsequently, she attended one of my seminars in Southern Oregon. In fact, I picked her up from her trailer home just north of San Francisco, and she rode with me to the seminar. We traveled with another woman I met in Nevada who was to be my San Luis Obispo sponsor. Devilla claimed that this woman was a witch who belonged to the Esalen Center in California. She even showed me written material with the woman's name. Devilla claimed she came along to protect me. After the seminar, I arranged for someone to drive Devilla on to the Portland area. There, she was scheduled to stay and work with Cisco Wheeler, a former government programmer. Little did I know at the time what that stay was going to do to Devilla, and her role in events to come.

My seminar, held outside of Zurich, went very well. People came from all over Europe. I missed Jonathan, who was only five-months old, terribly. On this trip, I was unusually homesick the entire time.

My Swiss partner and I had to start our trip to the Philippines by way of Munich, as our flight from Zurich was cancelled. On our way, we planned on stopping in Thailand so he could take care of some business. This proved to be a long trip, meandering across two continents. I always wanted to see Romania since that was the country of my maternal grandfather's birth. After flying through Austria and Hungary, I finally saw Romania. It was disappointing.

The Black Sea was not black at all. Turkmenistan was bleak, but Afghanistan was interesting. When we arrived in Kabul, my Swiss partner called it "Kabulshit," which I thought was humorous. Pakistan was more modernized than I anticipated.

When we arrived in Kashmir, I saw what I thought was a thunderstorm with violent lightening. Strangely, it remained in one place without moving. A few days later I learned that the Indian army had attacked and killed 160 rebels. What a lovely welcome to India!

Myanmar was exceptionally green and full of rice paddies, as was Thailand. I was not prepared for the overwhelming heat and humidity of Southeast Asia. I also was not prepared for the size of the roaches, or the food. In many cases, it appeared to be the same thing!

We stayed in Thailand for a while, arranging business ventures. The United States Navy was in town as well. My hotel stationed Thai soldiers on every floor as a security measure. They must have thought that I was in the military because whenever I passed them, they jumped up to salute me. I kind of liked it.

After leaving Thailand, we traveled through Cambodia where everything looked absolutely dead, and then on to Danang, Viet Nam. Here, I suddenly became emotionally overwhelmed, crying as if I had lost someone there, but I had not. I felt the pain and anguish of all the American and Vietnamese who died here so unnecessarily.

The purpose of that war was to test weapons for use on underground bases that could be used against the Illuminati. Years later, they tested the next generation of "smart" bombs in Iraq.

I met a man in Kentucky who was based in Thailand during the war. He told me that the Americans were testing burrowing nuclear weapons on the underground lairs of the Viet Cong. This man used to direct the strikes. I subsequently found out from another source that these "smart" weapons were the real cause for the illnesses often attributed to Agent Orange. In fact, Agent Orange does not exist.

The reason soldiers got sick and trees were defoliated was because of the radiation that leaked to the surface after a hit. These small tactical nuclear weapons burrowed into the Earth before exploding. The resultant radiation permeated the surface, causing extensive damage to people and plants. That also explains why the children of these soldiers were born with deformities. The radiation caused the sperm to mutate, and the soldiers' wives became sick from exposure to the radioactive poisons in their husbands' bodies.

Some soldiers found out about this and asked for the records to be released. They were taking the government to court. The records were kept in a vault in the F. Murrah Building in Oklahoma City. You know the rest!

We left Viet Nam, crossing over the South China Sea. We flew over Manila, one of the most corrupt and largest cities in the world with over 15 million people. Manila looks like someone took corrugated metal and loose pieces of wood, smashed them together, then dumped them in a heap.

Finally the time came to meet the Reverend who arranged for us to view the crystal. Our taxi took us to the seediest section of town, with raw sewage running in the streets. The building we stopped in front of looked dark, dank, and foreboding. The Reverend's name is also a color. He is an ex-American who runs an orphanage. He is a partner with another ex-American military man who lives in the valley on Mindanao where we were going.

The Reverend is an ill man who needs a nurse twenty-four hours per day. I was told that he pays off many government people as well as rebels on the southern islands. I was also told that he likes to poison people, get them arrested, and threaten them. All this was going through my mind when he invited us to dinner.

As we sat in a dark, damp, steamy, room, the Reverend told my Swiss partner that he was not welcome in the southern islands because he had an attitude with the local people on his first visit there. So, here I was, having dinner with a corrupt, unscrupulous individual who was antagonizing my partner, threatening him about what could happen to us in Mindanao, while my American guests were en route to Manila! I couldn't stop them now. We would have to face whatever was there, I realized, as I feigned eating.

The Reverend claimed he was my father during an Egyptian lifetime. As I was thinking that it was possible, I felt the abuse of the orphans, all male, in that building. I wondered why the Reverend had not returned to America in forty years. I wondered why he seemed to know so much about me. I wondered why I came, and if I would survive the trip.

That night, my Swiss partner and I spent the night in a dingy hotel that advertised sexual massages. In the morning, we went to the airport. We planned to greet the Americans, then fly together to the capital of the island of Mindanao, Davao City. Due to bad weather, one of our guests was delayed in San Francisco for the horrendous Philippine Airlines trip. She met us a day later in Davao City.

We met the others, and transferred to the domestic terminal for our flight to Mindanao. The airplane's bathrooms were filthy, overflowing with waste. The flight attendants spent much of the time smoking and applying make-up in the galley instead of attending to the passengers on the packed Airbus.

I sat directly behind Devilla. I noticed that something was terribly different about her. She seemed rather reserved, which I thought was from being tired from her long flight to Manila. Suddenly, she put an alien puppet dressed in a biker outfit on her hand. She affected an alien/biker voice, speaking "through" the puppet! This was my first clue that something happened to her at the home of the well-known programmer in Oregon.

In Davao City we checked into a circa World War II hotel that had never been updated. In the lobby, magazines dated 1967 were provided for the guests to read. They were in extremely good condition, so I assumed that they did not get much hotel business. At night, the electricity went out periodically, which is a common event in third world countries.

The next day we went shopping in town and exchanged money. It was hot and sticky all of the time. The wife of the ex-American military man was our escort. She was a native woman who owned a lot of land in the valley where we were going. She spoke English and Togalog, as well as the local dialect of her valley.

The following day, a huge, old, non-air-conditioned bus pulled up in front of the hotel. Soon we were on our way to the Maragusan Valley in eastern Mindanao. There were only the ten of us plus our hostess, and a few Filipino boys from the valley who were related to our hostess. We all had our own aisle of seats. The windows were open, letting in what precious breeze was available, mixed with dust and fumes from the winding gravel and dirt roads.

The three-hour trip through austere mountains included inclines and hairpin turns that the bus barely made. I help my breath as I observed the drops of hundreds of feet at the edge of these cliffs.

Just as I was about to give up hope of ever seeing a civilized building again, we pulled into a "resort" called Aguacan, hidden in the jungle surrounded by the huge mountains. The valley looked like it belonged on another planet. The resort had no hot water and little electricity. There were no phones, television, or radio reception. There were a total of ten of us, and we each were assigned a thatched-roof hut raised off the ground. Each hut had a small, primitive bathroom with a hole in the floor for a toilet. My bed greeted me with a gigantic dead roach the size of a Volkswagen. Lizards were on the walls and ceilings as well as prehistoric-proportioned insects that defied the senses.

The resort managers warned us about the poisonous plants, toxic insects, bats, rats, cats, and wild monkeys that bit. I thought that perhaps a huge dinosaur would pop up at any time! But, I was stuck here for the duration and was determined to make the best of it.

Devilla immediately started agitating everyone. She refused to join us for meals and stayed in her hut while we went on sightseeing excursions. When she did come with us, she was belligerent and rude. She claimed to have strep throat, and despite her nastiness, everyone tried to help her, even giving her our medicines. She constantly slipped papers into my hut from Cisco Wheeler describing deprogramming techniques as well as methods to program small children. Devilla said that this would trigger something in me.

In the meantime, I was keeping company with a woman who I met in my first seminar in Florida. The first time I saw her, I immediately recognized her as the Goddess I described in "Ritual in Red." She also was the girl used in my Montauk sexual programming. She came on the trip with an older woman. This girl had grown into a pretty woman, but she had a difficult life and broken marriage. Her husband infected her with an illness classified as incurable.

She had recently completed acupuncture school, and suggested that I come to her hut for a treatment. I became sexually aroused exactly as had happened at Montauk. We spent the rest of our time in the Philippines together, knowing that it was only for that short time that we would be together in this way. This was a form of closure after what we had been through.

Although I knew it was morally incorrect, I could not stop myself from ending this program that was running in my mind-pattern. It was like going through an obstacle course that I had to complete in order to get to my goal line which was with my wife Janet. I knew that I wanted to spend the rest of my life with Janet, and I had to get this garbage out of the way.

During daylight hours, we were taken to the jungle bridge where the crystal was kept resting over a stream, enclosed behind wooden doors in a grotto. The entire place was like something out of science fiction dinosaur movie. Only it was real. Strange carvings of unknown symbols decorated the flimsy bridge and the grotto doors. We were told that the crystal had allegedly been cared for here by mysterious natives for 48,000 years, and that it was believed to be a technological device left over from ancient Lemuria.

At that time, it was supposedly used for religious and programming purposes. The natives also said that they had one at their village where no one is ever allowed, and another one buried in a secret place that they would not yet reveal. Keep in mind that the Philippines is part of the original Lemurian continent. The ex-American military man explained that we had to acclimate to its energy before seeing it glow at night. It did have an effect on most of us. We all felt jittery and light-headed in its presence.

Our third trip to the stone was at night in the steamy, buggy jungle. Our guides were young, teenage Filipinos. Once darkness came, my Swiss partner would allow each of us, one by one, to view the stone after the initial group viewing. When the guides opened the wooden doors that protected the grotto, my jaw fell open when I viewed this amazing object. I knew that it was technology from another place. It definitely was not earthly. Even the way it glowed an eerie unearthly green into the jungle was something that I had never before or since experienced.

This is when the incident occurred with Devilla. She became belligerent toward everyone, telling us that this was a set-up. She claimed that what we were viewing was a movie set, and she would prove it to us. When her turn came to view the crystal, she reached in, rocked it off the pedestal, and knocked the 600 plus pound object into the stream below! We were all horrified. A terrible argument ensued amongst us and at her.

Then suddenly, a loud yelping came from the depths of the jungle. Unbeknownst to us, the mysterious natives were watching us, and had observed the desecration of their holy object! We were previously warned about their poisonous blow darts, and told that they thought nothing of killing white people. So, when they began to yelp and scream in a bloodcurdling manner, we ran for our lives.

I grabbed the hand of an elderly woman whom I knew to be my mother in another lifetime, and ran into the darkness. The guide in front of me was terrified. We crossed over rotted logs in streams. As we ran up mud staircases carved into the hillsides, I felt the dirt collapse under my feet, my hand still attached to that poor woman flying in the air behind me!

The guides were too afraid to stay on the path, so they cut through the jungle to race us to the truck that was our "limo" during our stay. With all of us safely on board, the truck screeched down the dirt road toward the village.

As soon as we reached the military man's house, I told Devilla to leave. I did not care how she got out, but I could no longer be responsible for her safety. In addition, she had already alienated everyone, and no one wanted to be in her presence. Her first opportunity to leave was the following day. She left with an elderly woman whose father was in ambassadorial service years before. Both of them deserved each other, although everyone realized that on another level, they were both performing actions exactly as they came there to do.

That night, there were mysterious flashes of light in the sky, similar to lightning, but without thunder. There were no storms. Suddenly, the wild monkeys in the jungle began to shriek in a bloodcurdling way, sounding like they were being brutally slaughtered. It was extremely frightening. No one slept that night between the noise, and our worry that the natives were coming to kill us.

The next morning as we sat at breakfast talking, the ground began to roll. My chair fell backwards, and I grabbed onto the table to prevent from cracking my skull open on the hard floor. We experienced a major earthquake with an epicenter on the north coast of Mindanao. Several people in a larger city there were killed. Constant aftershocks were continuous. Several days after that, a typhoon threw wind and rain at us on its way to Manila. Were these retributions from the energy of the crystal?

Many of us kept seeing the crystal mentally at the pineal gland. Physically, we could no longer go to see it. We were all upset by the sequence of events. We were only the second small group of white people ever allowed to view this magnificent crystal, and one of us had thrown it into the stream. What could the natives think of us? We concluded that we most likely would be the last group of white people to ever see the crystal for a long time to come.

Rebel activity near the valley was rampant. The day we left, two men were found beheaded. Two Europeans were kidnapped by Moslem separatists as our plane left Davao City. In Manila, the group boarded a flight back to the states. My Swiss sponsor and I had one more day in Manila. We were summoned to the Reverend's home, but we stalled, as the military man warned us that the Reverend might try to have us killed.

We waited nervously for our Thai Airlines flight back to Bangkok. We kept waiting for police or the military to pick us up on false charges. After all, this was the airport where Aquino was assassinated.

In Bangkok I became extremely ill. On rare occasions, I have a small amount of internal bleeding from my Montauk experience, but now I was literally hemorrhaging. I could hardly get off the bed in the hotel. I called Janet to tell her what was going on. She did some mental healing work on me, and I was better the next day. My trip home through Laos, Taiwan, and Japan was long and uneventful. I was glad to be out of Asia. Japan was a disappointment to me. The people were pushy, rude, and arrogant. The Tokyo area reminded me of a cross between New York City and Los Angeles.

I wanted to kiss the ground upon my return to America. Nothing seemed more beautiful than the sight of the Olympic Peninsula and

Puget Sound, Janet's home area. I still sensed the crystal in my brain calling to me. I seemed to have a strong connection with it. I felt like it was trying to tell me something. I continuously mentally reviewed the events of the past five weeks. Everything seemed like a dream, but I was used to that.

Several weeks later I received a fax from the Reverend berating me for what happened, blaming me for the injury to the crystal, then inviting me back to bring another group! What is wrong with that picture? He also said he had a tape of a conversation between my Swiss sponsor and myself in Zurich, although he would not explain further. This caused a rift between my Swiss sponsor and myself, as well, since I did not trust any of them now.

In the meantime, I was glad to be home. I vowed never to be away for such an extended length of time again. My children hardly knew me at all.

20

ALLIANCE EN FRANCE

We zipped down the winding French country roads at 175kph. I was in the front passenger seat of the black Saab with my fingers gripping the edge of my seat. I thought that it would be a strange way to leave the Earth after all I had been through. The driver, Piet, was a race driver in his youth. Piet is a Swiss friend whom I met a year earlier at the World UFO Congress in Zurich.

In the backseat was Rosemarie, Piet's companion. We had left Aarau early in the morning, driving through Basel on our way to the French border. We drove through the hills of the Jura district, then paralleled the Danube River and the German border. When traveling between European Union countries, passports are no longer required. We simply stopped briefly at the border marker, where no guards were present, then traveled into France.

We anticipated a thirteen-hour drive to the southwest French town of Caduoin, in the Dordogne region. A river of the same name flows through the area. This region is known for its magnificent wines and frois gras. Here, pilgrims come to retrace the footsteps of the Magdalene lineage. A church in Caduoin allegedly contains the handkerchief used to wipe the brow of Christ on his way to the cross. Pilgrims come from all over Europe to see the cloth and ask for intervention in their lives.

This area of France has superb underground springs that gush out everywhere. People stop on the side of the road to fill jugs of water to take home. Since the completion of the Chunnel, the tunnel under the English Channel that connects England and France, many British people come here to purchase old chateaux and to vacation.

Piet was taking me to see a several hundred years old chateau that was a mill at one time. The chateau was located on fifteen acres in a hilly section between Toulouse and Bordeaux, and thirty minutes from the quaint town of Bergerac. I drove part of the way, as I love driving a stick-shift on European roads. It was the start of the 1999 summer holiday season, and the roads were crowded.

By the time we got to the town, I was extremely tired after traveling from the states, through London, on to Switzerland, and then this thirteen-hour speed trip. We enjoyed a wonderful French dinner that energized me, and I became excited about the town. The people of southern France are known for their hospitality, good times, and generosity. Only the northern parts, particularly the Paris area, is considered arrogant and snobby.

Our hotel was almost one thousand years old, and was situated across a narrow stone street from a church monastery. My room was pleasantly decorated, considering the age of the building, and was painted pale blue with white trim. Although small, the bathroom was extremely modern. The hotel was once an inn for religious travelers.

That night, as I lay in bed reading, I felt a strange sensation in the room coming from the shuttered window. Looking up, I saw the images of three nuns by the window dressed in black and white habits. Their headdresses looked like wings with a pointed top, reminding me of "The Flying Nun," a 1960s television show.

Oblivious to my presence, I watched the three of them slowly walk in front of my bed and enter the bathroom. I heard clanking coming from the bathroom. I went in, but no one was there. Mentally, I blessed them, telling them to go to the violet or gold light.

The next day I told Piet about it. He laughed, saying that only monks and priests used to stay here. Perhaps I was a bit overtired, but he agreed to keep an open mind.

That night I talked to the nuns. They told me that they were murdered in that room by a priest who came to rape them, almost a century earlier. The priest, who lived in the monastery across the street, was never suspected. Instead, their murder was blamed on a pilgrim passing through the area. After that, I never saw the nuns again, although I sometimes felt a presence in the room.

A few days later, we went inside a small information bureau located in the town square.

Suddenly, Piet excitedly called me over to a wall display. There on the wall were photos taken years ago of visitors to the town. One of the photos showed three nuns dressed exactly as I had seen them in my room! I felt goose bumps all over.

We went to the chateau every day. On the land was a waterfall with an outcropping over the top of the waterfall that looked like a horse's head. The water rolled over the "nose" of the horse, continuing down to a pool that was built a long time ago. Piet knew the Swiss and English owners. They gave him permission to walk the land and enjoy the waterfall.

Piet brought an ancient, brass Chinese gong that was given to him by a friend. When he played the gong, nature literally paused. The vibrations were fantastically energizing, with the ability to send me directly into hyperspace. One afternoon, a few minutes after Piet played the gong, a lone French Mirage jet fighter swooped down directly over us and then took off! As far as we knew, there were no airforce bases anywhere close. Piet believes that the vibration of this ancient gong set off a blip on radar screens that the military instantly investigated.

Also on this property is a mysterious cave, hidden by natural growth. The cave's entrance is the exact shape of a Reptilian eye. Any photo taken from inside the cave looking out results in a picture that looks identical to a green lizard eye.

Pushing aside the underbrush to enter, I saw a dirt and rock floor. On the walls and ceiling were rock formations that resembled Reptilian forms. In the middle of the dark cave was evidence of a fire someone made for warmth or cooking a long time ago. Yet, there were absolutely no soot or fire marks anywhere in the cave.

Moving slowly back into the cave's interior, I saw that it narrowed and came to an end in a tiny area. In this tiny area were two slits in the rock wall that looked like nostrils. Placing my hand over the slits, I felt air moving out of them. My hands felt like they were over air-conditioning vents.

I decided to sit on some rock outcroppings from the dirt floor to mentally explore the cave from hyperspace. I immediately found myself deep underground in a large cavern filled with water. I saw a strange human-like creature with Reptilian features and slimy white skin. It called itself a "Mohan." It told me that in Atlantis I was responsible for creating an amphibian-hybrid using dolphin, human, and Reptilian genetics.

The Mohan continued, telling me that its species was ostracized by the three other groups, even though they carried their genes. It lived underground in this huge cavern where the water supply originated before coming to the surface. It said that I was responsible for leaving it there for safekeeping. It wanted to live on the surface but whenever any of its people came to the surface, the humans killed them. When they ventured further underground, they were hunted by the Reptilians. The dolphins could not live in the same environment either, so they were forced to live in isolation forever. Suddenly, I was pushed back into my body. I felt chilled, depressed, sad, and lonely from the experience. I needed to get out of the cave.

I later learned that the word "Mohan" is of East Indian origin. Its meaning implies deception or falsehood. I believe that these call themselves this because they live an artificial existence in a place that is false for them. They were deceived into thinking it would be a safety area. The name is appropriate for them.

After the cave, we walked the property, marveling at the beautiful bamboo forest the previous owner planted. There were huge manmade ponds stocked with fish, with a porcupine wandering around them.

Above the hill behind the waterfall was a stand of tall white birch trees. Walking over to it, I suddenly was transported back in time to a ceremony that I conducted on this spot. I told Piet and Rosemarie that I remembered transporting a section of the top of an Atlantean pyramid to this area. I had it crushed into little pieces and buried in this stand of birch trees as a remembrance of the migration after the sinking of the continent. The pyramid top was white and sparkly.

Piet suggested that I dig in a spot that I thought would be appropriate. So, with my shoe and bare hand, I dug in the rich black soil right in the middle of the circle of white birch trees. Within moments, and only a few inches down, white, shiny rock appeared. I dug a few feet away and more of the crushed white stone appeared. It confirmed my vision and memory. This pyramid top was crushed and placed here over 12,000 years ago to recreate the pyramid energy signature for the future. I felt I had come full circle by finding it again.

The land was also covered by butterfly bushes. Butterflies of all types and colors flock to this place. Butterflies hold magnetism for the Earth. Given the presence of the crushed pyramid top, I was not surprised that they were here, and neither was I surprised at the Mirage fighter's appearance.

I felt an energetic connection from this land in France to the area in Mindanao where the amazing green crystal is located. I also felt a connection to the vortex in Wanaque, New Jersey where I went with my friend, Bryan Williams, and his girlfriend, Sandra. Bryan and I share the same birthday. He takes amazing digital photos of Reptilian creatures that exit from this vortex on DuPont land. These creatures called themselves "Endorrans."

This property is close to the famous castle Rennes-le-Chateau where mysterious legends about the true nature of Christianity are kept hidden. Rennes-le-Chateau sits atop a major entrance to the inner Earth. This entrance has been protected by the Catholic Church and elite families for centuries.

The property is also close to the small nation of Andorra, located in the Pyrenees. This entire area of France, Spain, and Andorra is crisscrossed with caves and underground tunnels that were once home to the original Magdalene travelers who came here 2,000 years ago.

The true origins of the Magdalene lineage and the real truth behind Christianity have their proof in Rennes-le-Chateau. Artifacts and scrolls from ancient Israel are kept there, and the hybrid Reptilians use this castle for ritual and ceremony.

My wife, Janet, has her roots in this place. She is of the French-Magdalene lineage, directly descended from the Duke of Savoy and the Mourglia family. Her people eventually became the Waldensians. They left France for Uruguay, before going on to the United States, settling in the Ozarks of Southwestern Missouri.

Symbolically, that area is identical to Southwestern France. Both areas are crisscrossed with mysterious caves and tunnels, and are located in the southwest of their region. Both have French settlers and wine businesses. Both areas remain isolated. At times, when standing on the land of the chateau, I could feel Janet's energy. The beautiful roses reminded me of her. I knew that someday, all of us would return here to live and work.

The chateau and carriage house are in excellent condition. Piet and I know that it would make an excellent summer spot for seminars. This particular chateau is for sale. When some English people stopped to look at it, Piet told them that it was sold! As of this writing, Piet is actively raising the funds necessary to purchase this land and chateau. One day it will be accomplished.

On the long drive back to Switzerland we ran out of gas. This has never happened to Piet or me before. I symbolically understood that I was to stay there. In this place, we could live and work. We no longer needed to travel. Our search "ran out of gas."

On the flight back to London, and then to the states, I felt that I was being prepared for something. I now know that I was being fortified for what was coming next in my life.

21

ILLUMINATI AGENT

The story of Johannes von Gruber is more complex than I have previously shared. Although he was married with two children and a wife in Heidelberg, he also had a mistress by the name of Rosie. She was in her 30's when Johannes left Germany for the states and his impending participation in the Philadelphia Experiment.

Rosie was a spy who was well-trained by the Nazis and Illuminati in sexual magic, drugs and narcotics, weapons and silent execution, and deception and disinformation. She had no problem befriending unsuspecting targets with her charm and sexuality, and then killing them in cold blood. Rosie reported directly to Johannes, who actually had several such robotical killers in his entourage. In turn, Johannes reported directly to the German High Command.

Rosie was upset when Johannes left on a mission so secret that he could not even tell her about it. With Johannes gone, she was an open target. She knew that other German commanders would use her services, then throw her to the wolves, so she kept a low profile. After several months when Johannes did not return, everyone assumed that he was dead. Orders were given to eliminate Rosie because she knew too much. So, she was called to an Illuminati ritual in the mountains of Southern Germany where she was asked to perform in a blood-ritual. Her superiors failed to mention that she was the sacrifice.

They kept her soul essence contained in the astral levels until they needed her. In the late 1940s she was brought into a body in the United States. Her training as an assassin and destroyer was reinforced, and her sexuality was kept open. Her controllers involved her in drugs and demonology, finally placing her into the Monarch mind-control program. Her mission was to find and control programmed males who either left the program, became uncontrollable, or were considered a liability to the Illuminati. Her mission was to remove them from their current environment, download old programming, retrain them with new orders, and destroy their family and business connections and ties.

Given a new name and identity, Rosie 2 was turned loose on the unsuspecting world. They assigned two males as her assistants. One posed as her husband, the other as her innocent, Asian friend, who initially made contact with me in March, 1998 when he called for a phone consultation. He said he bankrupted his parents by using all of their credit cards, then using one to pay off the other in a revolving credit scheme. He also claimed to be a twenty-seven year old virgin, a claim I now know to be false. He invited me to present a seminar in Orlando, Florida the upcoming June.

One of the attendees was Rosie 2, who claimed to be of Cherokee, Black Foot, and Irish descent. After the seminar, I had a migraine, and she insisted on massaging my head. In the process, she stuck her hands down my shirt, pinching my nipples. This was one of the techniques used to program me at Montauk. Looking back, I now realize in that instant she triggered our connection.

After I returned home, she began leaving messages saying that she was fascinated with me, and wanted to see me at my next Orlando seminar in September 1998. She claimed that she was the one who really put the seminar together, not her friend. During her calls to me, Rosie 2 insinuated that she "knew" who I was. She said that I would be divorcing my wife, Janet, and that I would belong to the world. With her help, I would become famous.

One night during the September seminar in Orlando, Rosie 2 came to my room. She again told me that I would be divorcing Janet and my children would be taken away from me again. Tired after a long workday, I became emotional, and her "comfort" became sexual. Then, she told me she had to leave at 4:00AM to do "something."

She claimed to be 36 years old, but her hands and face belied her true age, which was closer to 50. She claimed to run houses in the area for people in need of a second chance. She said it was non-profit, but she refused to take any state or federal aid. I thought that was strange. I found out two years later that her houses were reputed to be revolving doors for sex and drugs which supplied her with both, earning a lot of unreported cash.

After that, I came to Florida every two to three months. She was always there and we always had wild, incessant sex. In my mind, I knew it was wrong. I loved my wife, Janet with all my heart. I knew I had no intentions of leaving her. But, I could not stop the sexual activity with

Rosie 2. She knew all of the trigger words that activated destructive programmed behavior in me that I never knew existed.

I drank and smoked more, and wanted sex all of the time. I felt like she had control over my mind and body. It was if I had two distinct personalities. Simply being with her or hearing her voice activated a part of me. Over a year's time, she gradually took over the Florida seminars and told me I would become "Emperor of the Planet." She said that she was a Reptilian and proud of it. I personally saw her shapeshift several times into a Reptilian, a cat-like being, and an old hag. I was shocked, but not afraid.

Sometimes she called me at home in the middle of the night, keeping me on the line for several hours. I heard her screaming obscenities, but I never knew to whom. Then at some point in the conversation, she often started to moan and cry, asking me questions that I could not understand. I always felt rage and hostility towards her and wished that she would go away forever.

She constantly flattered me, always telling me how beautiful my body was. She claimed to be capable of multiple orgasms, and it was common for her to have six or seven in one session. I now believe that these were faked. These sessions seemed to be designed to keep me under control. Sometimes, she even said she left her body and saw me as a lion. Eventually, I even felt and saw myself shapeshift into a winged lion. On a trip with me to Switzerland, she told Piet that she was a programmed sex slave and could feel nothing sexually.

I had terrible migraines when I was with her. Out of desperation I started taking some pills that she told me would help them. When I could not sleep, she gave me something for that. Soon, it seemed that she was popping pills in my mouth several times during the day, and eventually throughout the night while I was sleeping. I always asked her what they were, but she would never tell me. She only said that she had a doctor in Florida that gave her prescription drugs to help her clients. She said that she told him about me, and based on that, he gave her things to help me. I wonder if she said trigger words, or gave me other drugs, that produced the migraines in the first place. This "doctor" was an older Southeast Asian man whose name was a four-letter curse word in English. She always paid him in cash.

In the summer of 1999, Janet and I took six boys to Disney World. It was to be a wonderful family trip with my children that would probably never happen again. Rosie 2 arranged for our airport transportation, hotel, and another seminar to help pay for the trip.

The hotel where Rosie 2 booked us turned out to be sleazy and dirty. I now believe that this was designed to create dissension amongst my family. The hotel air-conditioning stopped functioning soon after we arrived. The outside temperature was 100 degrees with equal humidity. The boys were ready to mutiny. Then, Rosie 2 came to the rescue with her supposed husband, moving us to a better hotel with air-conditioning.

This was her standard modus operandi for my entire relationship with her. She created horrendous circumstances, then "rescued" me from it, always looking like a heroine. She never wanted money for her efforts, so she said. During our stay, she cornered Janet alone in her room. Claiming to be "psychic," she told Janet that Janet and I would get a divorce. She told Janet that Janet would be the one to leave me. She also said that she had no interest in me except for my healing work, and that if she wanted me, she would have me, but she did not want me. Janet was stunned and upset by the conversation, but because of Rosie 2's apparent support of my work, decided to wait to form her opinion.

After we returned home, she befriended Janet via phone calls and email, promising to enhance my career and re-establish Janet whenever she was ready. Janet had taken a sabbatical five years prior to have and raise our children. Jonathan was only a few months old when Rosie 2 befriended Janet. Janet was recovering from major surgery, taking care of the baby and Zachary, then three, and the older boys, plus trying to keep up with our growing business. For these reasons, she welcomed Rosie 2's help without asking too many questions. Unbeknownst to Janet, I was continuing to react to Rosie 2's threats and demands. She started visiting my home, and decided that she would call herself an equal business partner.

Since Janet could not travel because of our small children, Rosie 2 began to travel with me. She convinced Janet that she was a lesbian, so her traveling with me was not an issue. She told Janet that she would increase sales, find new sponsors, canvas bookstores, arrange events, manage product sales, and generally increase business. Even though it was a financial strain, we expected to see an increase in revenue to justify the additional expense.

Janet was still unaware that Rosie 2 was threatening and drugging me while pretending to be her friend. She never provided us with receipt books as we requested, and we later learned that she was skimming cash from our sales. She kept the household in a constant state of chaos and confusion. Whenever Janet tried to reconcile the books with her, she changed the subject and focused on other issues.

From the fall of 1999 to July 2000, we traveled extensively together, with almost no time apart. When we were not on the road together, she stayed at my home, claiming that it was less expensive than sending her home to Florida. Knowing how much Janet and I both hated the traveling, she convinced us that if she kept me on the road for a year or so, my name would be so well known that I could quit traveling.

I was with her more than my own family. We traveled all across the United States from Florida to Maine, from Texas to California to Alaska. We went across Latin America from the Panama Canal to Lima, from Santiago to Buenos Aires. In Europe I was everywhere from Spain to Switzerland, and Norway and Sweden, and even across Iceland and Greenland.

My sponsors in Norway, Germany, and Switzerland were outraged by her nastiness, and by how she controlled me. They thought that she was going to kill me. Many people tried to warn me, but I could not hear them.

Once we went to a small town in what was once East Germany to present a seminar. The building where we stayed was built over an old, World War II concentration camp. The room we were given was bloodstained and dirty. The lights flashed on and off by themselves. Everyone in the compound had nightmares, headaches, and agitation. Rosie 2 told me she liked the place and felt at home. As usual, she alienated everyone there.

Everywhere we went she consistently fired my promoters and ruined my business. She trashed me to people, calling me a womanizer and sex maniac. We fought constantly, and horribly. She always threatened to leave, but never did. She carried a gun and told me that she had killed people. She claimed to be pregnant twice, once even saying she was carrying twins, then mysteriously miscarried both times. She claimed to have had double breast cancer with one-half of one breast removed and three-fourths of the other one removed, followed by reconstructive surgery, but turned up with breast implants that I now realize was paid for with the cash she skimmed from us!

22

TANGO IN ARGENTINA

In February 2000, I was scheduled to take a trip to South America before traveling on to Europe to meet Rosie 2 in Zurich. She was going to be introduced to my European market and sponsors. Waiting for the taxi to take me to the airport that night, horrible waves of fear flooded through me. I knew that I must not get on that plane. Something inside said that if I went to Argentina alone, I might not come back.

I had scheduled my trip to take me to Buenos Aires, where I knew that I was destined to meet my "double." Years before, in the 1970s, I knew of a Stewart Swerdlow who lived in Santa Monica, on San Vicente Boulevard. In 1980, I actually went up to the building, but was too nervous to go inside. He was, is, another me.

I have been told that I have at least two alternate selves from parallel universes here as a result of the Montauk Project. One was in Los Angeles (L.A.), the other in Buenos Aires (B.A.). The "double" in Los Angeles felt benevolent, while the one in Buenos Aires was definitely Nazi-Illuminati. The thought flashed through my mind that he would kill me.

So, within an hour of the taxi service picking me up, I cancelled that portion of my trip, rescheduling my flight directly to Spain and from there, on to Zurich. As soon as I cancelled the South American segment, a great weight lifted from my shoulders. I was happy and comfortable again. Never before, or since, have I cancelled a trip in such a way.

In Europe, nobody liked Rosie 2, and our meetings with sponsors in Switzerland, Germany, and Norway were disasters. Everyone clearly saw how she manipulated me. At this point, I was like a robot that did as commanded. Students and clients thought that she was a prostitute from the way that she dressed and acted.

By the time we arrived in Stockholm for the final leg of the trip home, she was a nasty, manipulating bitch. She watched everything I did, questioned me about everyone with whom I spoke, and was constantly popping pills in my mouth.

As soon as we returned to the states, Rosie 2 persuaded Janet to reschedule the trip to South America even though we were almost broke. She told Janet she was going to network me there, and if I did not go, our marriage would be over. This time, Rosie 2 would go along to "protect me," she told Janet. During this time, April 2000, Rosie 2 started telling me that she would put me in sex movies as a porno star. This is a well-known programming protocol. She tried to convince me that I was bisexual, and even started placing ads on the Internet for group sexual partners, against my wishes.

Duncan Cameron came over for dinner the day we were scheduled to leave for South America, because Rosie 2 wanted to check him out. The weather was so awful, with torrential rain and wind, that I thought all flights would be cancelled.

Literally five minutes before we were scheduled to leave, the taxi company called to say its car was stuck in traffic and they were unable to pick us up. So, Duncan volunteered to take us to the airport. The ride was slow with poor visibility. Duncan's small car was washed over by the wake of other vehicles many times. The highway was like gushing rapids, and it was dark by the time we arrived. The rain had stopped, but thunderstorms were in the area. Privately, Duncan told me that he would be with me energetically, and to call on him if I needed help.

Immediately upon boarding the plane, Rosie 2 popped pills in my mouth. When I woke, we were at the Panama Canal. I remember thinking that it looked zig-zaggy instead of straight. The next thing I remember was looking at two smoking volcanic peaks in Ecuador. I remembered reading about the eruptions in the newspaper. Finally, we were in Lima, Peru. The coastline reminded me of California. We went shopping at some little tourist shops. I found a cute pair of llama statues, and she bought obscene sexual carvings that she was going to give as gifts.

As we flew over the Nazca plains. I strained to see the figures etched in the ground. Rosie 2 seemed uninterested in them. I could barely make out any images, and wondered what all the fuss was about them. I knew that they were created by the ancient Lemurians. This coastline was at the edge of that continent. The Lemurians loved to use the Earth as a canvas. They like to hover above the plateau to admire the artwork carved into the stone ground. These depictions are Reptilian archetypes, each one representing a quality of being for their culture. No wonder Rosie 2 seemed to not care – she probably had seen them many times before.

Santiago, Chile had the most breathtaking mountainous scenery in the world, a cross between the Swiss Alps and the Rockies, with a bit of the Los Angeles basin. The only other places that come close to this awesome sight are Greenland and Iceland.

I sat alone at a bar while Rosie 2 went to the bathroom. The woman behind the bar, whom I did not know, called me over in Spanish to ask if I would like to read the local paper. When I politely declined, she turned to a large article with pictures about the Chupracabra. This is a Spanish term for "goat-sucker," a legendary creature reported recently in the Caribbean and southern United States that attacks animals.

The Chupracabra supposedly bites them, then completely sucks out their blood and sometimes a few major organs. The woman told me that this had never happened in Chile until recently, and now they were being seen all over the country. She made a point of showing me this article, even though she supposedly did not know me.

Rosie 2 came out of the bathroom to say that a strange man entered the women's restroom, calling her name. She said we should leave the area immediately.

Later, while sitting in the airport waiting area, my name was called over the loudspeaker. We went to the information desk and a well-dressed man behind the counter gave me our boarding passes, directing us to the flight gate for Buenos Aires. I noticed that no one else was called. All the other passengers had to wait on a line at the gate desk. Our seats were in the last row at back of the plane.

The scenery of the Andes between Chile and Argentina was spectacular. I thought about a 1970s movie about a crash in this area where the survivors had to eat the dead passengers to survive. The region seemed too beautiful for such a sinister event to occur. But, many magnificent sites all over the world have been the scenes of horrendous, diabolical activities.

Buenos Aires felt like home. As soon as I set foot on Argentine soil, I felt like I had returned home. Like many times before, Rosie 2 found a male cabdriver at the airport who agreed to take us anywhere for little money. These drivers were more like private chauffeurs, rather than cabdrivers.

The hotel in town where we were scheduled to stay turned out to be a gay tryst center. While the driver waited downstairs, and we went to our room, I told Rosie 2 that I could not stay there. Rosie 2 wanted to stay, but I refused. Leaving our luggage at the hotel, the driver found us another, more modern hotel with a vacancy. I stayed there while the driver took Rosie 2 to retrieve our luggage. She returned with bloody hands. She told me that the desk clerk was nasty to her, so she jumped over the counter and punched him in the mouth. I was horrified. Of course there were no witnesses to this, and I now believe that she fabricated the entire story to keep me in line.

We must have walked over fifty miles during our few days in Buenos Aires. I never asked anyone for directions, I simply knew how to find our destinations. We went all over the city, even to the beach where I saw Uruguay across the water.

The Presidential Palace was a pink color. As we sat in front of it, I continuously flashed on blood-rituals in the basement in which I had participated. I kept reliving the scenes over and over. Then, I flashed back to the previous month at a conference in Houston when during amorous climaxes with Rosie 2, I saw myself change into a golden, winged lion. But what did this have to do with here and now?

My answer came the next day when we walked to the Congress Building, directly opposite the Presidential Palace in the Plaza de Mayo. Surrounding that building on every side were statues of golden, winged lions! I could not take my eyes off them. We must have been there for hours. While I stared at them, Rosie 2 went down the street to buy sexy leather outfits.

That night in our hotel room, we heard extremely loud screaming and moaning from the next room. Earlier in the day we saw a couple entering that room with long, rifle-looking bags. We now heard a man yelling at the top of his lungs in Spanish. Then he moaned, stopped for a while, then started again. Rosie 2 laughed maniacally, saying that the woman was a dominatrix and she was torturing the man in a prolonged journey to orgasm. She said that she wanted to do that to me, saying I would like it. From what I heard next door, I did not agree.

That weekend was Easter. Rosie 2 told me that the following Easter, she was going to marry me. I would divorce Janet, put her in a mental institution, and give my children away. As she laid out her plans, a part of me woke up to realize that I had to get away from this evil witch.

One evening as I looked closely at her she intently stared back. Suddenly, her face shifted into an ugly Reptilian hag. I almost lost my breath as I recoiled, then looked again. She was grinning as her face returned to a human female shape. I did not say a word about it and neither did she. Inside I was screaming. I wanted so badly to be with Janet and the boys. But we were off to Los Angeles the next day.

23

MYSTERY MAN & COMPANY

In 1999, one of the attendees at a San Luis Obispo, California, seminar was a medical professional from the Los Angeles area. I will call him George. George lived a fast life. He drove speedboats, owned a Porsche, piloted planes, and had an avante garde chiropractic practice in the San Fernando Valley. I immediately recognized his Montauk/Monarch programming signature. I liked him, and we soon became friends.

During a private session with George, I saw past tragedy and deep layers of programming within him. He could easily have been an assassin. He told me about his memories in another reality where he was called upon to do secret clean-up work for the government. He was exceptionally familiar with high-powered weapons, and actually had spent time in this reality in government service. He also invented various unconventional devices, including medical ones.

George introduced me to a well-known sex-slave who has gone public with her story. I also met her male handler, a well-known researcher of N.W.O. material.

So, here we all were in Los Angeles—myself, with my older, demonic female controller, and a red-haired sex-slave with her older male handler. At the time, I did not put the pieces together. I chastise myself now because I might have been able to spare myself and my loved ones a year of grief and aggravation.

Eventually, George began sponsoring and promoting me in the Los Angeles area. In January 2000, I did a great seminar at the Sportsmen's Lodge in Studio City. My favorite actress, Linda Grey, attended. She played "Sue Ellen" on the globally known television show, *Dallas*. Rosie 2 attended as my manager, alienating me from almost everyone there.

After the seminar, George and his live-in girlfriend took Rosie 2 and myself to the Integratron. This building, located in the middle of the desert, is close to the Twenty-Nine Palms Air Base. It was the creation of George von Tassel in the 1950s. He claimed to be a contactee who was given information by aliens to build this tower-like structure for the purpose of rejuvenating the human body.

On the way to the Integratron, we stopped in Joshua Tree National Park. There, I felt like I was on the surface of the moon. Trails and caves not publicly traveled were everywhere. George and his girlfriend took us down one of these trails to some caves in a cliff. Inside were petroglyphs and wall symbols that looked quite ancient. One of these caves housed a domed ceiling with a starburst painted at the peak of the dome. George told me to stand under it with my crown touching the starburst. The ceiling was low enough to do this. Stupidly, I followed directions. Immediately, I felt dizzy and sick, and had to return to the truck.

Next, we visited an ex-New York promoter of mine who now lived with the woman purchasing the Integratron. Together, we drove to the tower. Standing in the center of the structure to feel the energy, I knew that this was really built to create a vortex for Reptilian entry onto the Earth plane, much like a Star Gate.

The woman purchasing the Integratron asked me for building instructions to complete the structure. She explained that after the death of George von Tassel, most of the instructions to complete it were confiscated by the government. My answers confirmed what she had seen on some private documents.

Then, she and my ex-promoter literally whisked me away to Giant Rock a few miles into the desert. George von Tassel actually lived under this rock in a complex of rooms while the tower was being built. After his death, the government bulldozed the entrance saying that it was too dangerous for the public. I saw that it is an entrance to the inner Earth, and particularly to the underground Reptilian "nests" which are abundant under the Mojave Desert.

Over the next several months, George sponsored several seminars in the Los Angeles area. He was assisted by one of his clients, the wife of a major studio ex-vice-president. Rosie 2 befriended this woman, then attempted to create problems between her, George, Janet, and myself. This was akin to throwing everyone into a blender and turning it on. We all suffered.

While in California, Rosie 2 targeted a remote viewer who also presented global seminars and lectures. She threatened to destroy me and work with him if I did not do what she said. She told me that both he and I were being groomed for a major position in the Illuminati world, but only one of us could get it. She always pitted people against each other. I am sure that she slept with him, too, as well as anyone else she needed to use. As the months went on, and I plotted my future a la Rosie 2, my seminars and lectures dwindled to nothing. I was penniless and my marriage was in shambles.

Next, Rosie 2 arranged for the two of us and Preston Nichols to accompany George and his client on a visit to the Montauk Base. In addition, George brought an actress who was the wife of a major television drama series star. This woman was chronicling George's life for a possible book and movie.

On our first visit to the base with this group, because of the pouring rain, Preston and I waited in the car right outside of the gates. Rosie 2 helped the others to sneak onto the compound. Preston and I saw a white pick-up truck with California plates slowly drive past us as the male driver looked into our vehicle. He then drove to the gate in front of us, turned around, then parked on the opposite side of the road a few yards behind us. He never left his truck, and drove off after about thirty minutes.

The next day was sunny and beautiful. We all returned to the base, sneaking in the back entrance along a dirt path. We saw reconstruction going on by the Army Corps of Engineers. They were tearing down buildings and bulldozing others. We ran and hid all over the compound, avoiding white patrol vans that slowly maneuvered on the base roads.

Rosie 2 took me into an old building in terrible disrepair where I was kept as a child. Although I resisted, she insisted that I enter. Immediately, my heart started to violently flutter. I could not breathe as scenes of the past flooded my mind and emotions. This building was where "advanced" children were kept. I was in charge of them, although I was only a teenager myself at the time. I rushed out, over the road and up a wooded hill to a nearby radar tower. I narrowly missed being seen by a white van.

We gathered under the tower, deciding to go to the fence by the woods. We could not get through the barbed wire. We had to walk along a road near some deserted buildings. That is when we were caught!

A white pick-up truck on patrol slowly drove up in front of us. The driver was a young man working on the reconstruction project. Rosie 2 went alone to his window to speak to him. The rest of us thought we would be arrested for sure!

Rosie 2 returned to say the driver would not report us as long as we left immediately the way we entered. We practically ran to the exit hole in the gate. I now realize that Rosie 2 "knew" this man, and obviously had authority to be there. Anyone found on the Montauk Base is arrested, or at minimum is unceremoniously escorted off with threats.

Later that week, George's client flew back to California, and the remaining four of us drove up to Maine, George's birthplace. We took a speedboat to the islands off the coast of Portland. In 1976, a British "friend" whom I met in the Middle East took me to Peak Island, a hotbed for Illuminati ritual and ceremony. The homes are owned by wealthy, Northeastern elite who spend summers here. I experienced strange things in one of these houses that year, and now here I was again.

George took us to old, disintegrating military bunkers that were situated on most of these outlying islands. Supposedly designed to defend the harbor from invading fleets, they were all suspiciously built away from the shoreline without view of the water. The vast underground areas were all cemented over, similar to the Montauk Base. George remembered being here as a child. He was trying to recapture buried memories. The places felt foreboding and evil to me.

As usual, Rosie 2 was having a ball. While in Maine, she even purchased a wedding ring/engagement set for us for one thousand dollars cash. There was an even more expensive set that she loved for five thousand dollars. She planned on having her supposed husband wire her the money for that set, but it was sold when she went back to purchase it. She insisted that I tell everyone that I had purchased it for her.

On our last night, we went to the gates of the Brunswick Air Force Base. There is no doubt in my mind that this area was and is being used for ritual and ceremony. The city has a dense, negative energy all over it. It was here that George's younger brother was hit and killed by a car that followed their school bus for miles when George was a child. George's father never pressed charges against the killer. His mother was sent for strange electrical treatments in Boston, and had a strange relationship with the doctor involved. The way the accident was described, it appeared to be an Illuminati set-up. Only a couple of years prior to that, on the exact same spot, George was almost killed by a speeding driver. Apparently, the earlier failed sacrifice was later successfully carried out.

Through George, I met a woman who gave my name to a friend at Paramount Studios who worked for LaVar Burton. They were developing a project about the creation of life on Earth. The story line was fiction based on truth. They called, wanting to base a character on me. Then they told me about a woman who was involved in the production—who "coincidentally" just happened to have been my deprogrammer and controller for a number of years in the early 1990s!

I told LaVar that I did not think this woman would be happy about my involvement. I was correct! She threatened the studio with a lawsuit, then called my home to threaten me about giving out any more information. The project was stopped, and I was blamed for it.

A few months after our trip to Maine, George revealed that he had secretly called my ex-deprogrammer and interrogated her about me. He taped the conversation, and his client transcribed it. This had happened prior to our trip to Montauk and Maine. He only told me about it when I returned to California. I was extremely disappointed. Once again, I felt used and manipulated. How could he pretend to be my friend while secretly talking to someone who openly threatens to destroy me?

George was obviously something more sinister than I realized. All of these people were part of a gigantic staged Illuminati play. Perhaps they consciously knew, or perhaps they were living out their programming. Either way, it was not a pretty picture. I had nothing more to do with any of them, except Rosie 2. She was still my controller.

It was soon after these events that I wound up in Anchorage, Alaska with Rosie 2 in her final attempt to remove me from my family and society. Shortly after that I was back on Long Island being welcomed into the loving arms of my God-sent wife and my wonderful children. If it were not for them, my parents, my sister, and a few good friends, I would now be in Illuminati isolation.

24

THE END OF ROSIE 2

Wherever we went, Rosie 2 kept me food and sleep deprived, along with the pills she constantly popped into my mouth. When I returned home in July 2000, I had eighteen needle marks on my back. She kept the hotel rooms extremely hot, then extremely cold. She constantly sprayed "perfumes" throughout our hotel rooms, claiming that it covered the smell of her cigarettes. She called me a fraud, and told people that she was my next wife. She said that Janet was insane and should be committed, and our children taken from her. She constantly berated my entire family and did her best to isolate me from any support system that I had.

She told me that my children were lost to me and I would never see them again. She blocked phone calls from my family and threatened to kill them. She had someone call my sister in the middle of the night claiming to be me. This person told my sister that I had taken the drug ecstasy and was about to kill myself.

She kept me in Anchorage, Alaska, opening a bank account with me under the name "Rosie 2 Swerdlow." She tried to get me an Alaska driver's license, and wanted to rent an apartment for us. I knew I needed to escape before I was lost to my family forever. While on the way from Anchorage back to her home in Orlando, we stopped in New York City, and I told her that I had to see my children. She told me to call her every day and reject everything my family did to make me stay.

When I walked through the door of my house, I felt like I was waking up from a coma. I felt like a character out of the movie "Pleasantville," witnessing a black and white world turning into color. Only then did I realize what was done to me and my family. To my surprise, Janet welcomed me with open arms. According to Rosie 2, Janet was the one who stole money from me, set up secret bank accounts, and had numerous affairs while I was gone. Every day, Rosie 2 repeated these things to me over and over again, drilling me on my responses and feelings until she could elicit the reaction she wanted with a simple glance.

During my last absence, Janet called everyone involved with Rosie 2 and us, both professionally and personally, collected facts, and wrote them down. Even though I had been up all night, which at this point was not unusual, we went over everything. Over the course of several weeks, Janet worked with me to deprogram all that Rosie 2 had done to me, including bringing in all my family and closest friends and business associates until I began to come back to what is "normal" for me. It actually took quite a few months until I had any semblance of my normal self.

As the effects of the drugs wore off, I was in shock over what I had gone through, but realized that enough of the "real me" was present so that no one could ever completely control me as had been done at Montauk. Even with the drugs and mind-control techniques, on some level I consciously maintained enough of my identity to get myself out of the situation and back home to my loved ones where I belong. Rosie 2 managed to find my weak areas and magnify my fears, using them against me. But, that was all that she could do. She could not and did not reach the deepest part of my soul that contains my abilities and information.

Rosie 2 damaged me on many levels. She skimmed cash from all my seminars, then kept a chunk of the profits as her "pay," plus, Janet gave her 10% of the gross as well as paid for all her travel expenses. She stole my cameras, notes, clothing, inventory, and self-esteem. She even stole my only Soviet passport photo of my grandmother taken in the early 1900s that is irreplaceable. She took a photo album containing a photo of my first government deprogrammer and an autographed picture of an actor client of mine who had passed away, and some of Janet's photo albums. She took a $10 radio that I loved. I found out that she has a rap sheet as long as my arm. We notified the police and FBI in New York and Florida, for whatever that is worth. She even told me that she had a warrant out for her arrest in Florida on an issue that she was vague about. She said that we would have to be on the lam for a couple of years.

She has targeted several other people while she was with me. She wanted to sleep with them, then take their money and businesses while appearing to be their partner and promoter. These include author David Moorehouse, Global Sciences Congress organizer Dean Stonier[1], and author David Icke. I warned all of them, but only David Icke responded. Now it is their problem.

She has roped into her sphere of influence Arizona Wilder, Brian Desborough, and Royal Adams. She takes people in by her fake Southern charm and false promises. She preys on wealthy older people, or poor people with marketable potential. Her ultimate aim is their destruction.

Death means nothing to her. She prays to many demons, among them one named Abraxis. She even told me how she killed infants. She drew blood and semen from my body to perform sexual magic. She is a demonic plague from the depths of hell controlled by the Reptilian Illuminati. Keep your eyes out for a 5' 2" dyed-blonde, artificially created size 0, with tanned, wrinkled skin and a wide nose. She has an affected Southern drawl and speaks inappropriately. She likes to wear as little clothing as possible. She loves to show-off her double dolphin tattoo over her rear end that I believe is a visual trigger. These types of body-markings are often used in programming. She claims to be in her late 30s but she was born in the 1940s. She is armed and dangerous.

She had information on me that could only have come from the Illuminati themselves. She practiced typical Illuminati techniques-she took the truth and twisted it to suit her own purposes. She kept me in a constant state of confusion. She would tell me a story, and when I related it back, she would tell me that it never happened, or it happened a different way.

She made me tell her information that I had never told another living soul. She practiced the mind-control technique of divide and conquer. She separated me from my wife, my family, my children, my home. She kept me on the road just to keep me on the road. She told me I had seminars scheduled, and when I arrived, I found out there were no seminars. Then she blamed them on my sponsors and destroyed my relationships with them. She took nude photos of me and said she was going to get me into pornography. Debasing activities are another way to break a personality for programming.

I am revealing all of this because I would not want anyone else to fall victim to her schemes and plotting. Also, in case anything happens to me or my family members, she should be the number one suspect. I am also revealing this information because I want everyone to know that even with everything that I know, I was once more a victim. However, using what I know, I refused to remain a victim.

The year 2000 was not easy. My finances were at their worst, yet my feelings about myself are at my best. She did not accomplish her mission.

She did not destroy me, my marriage, my family, or my ability to disseminate information. My family life is stronger than ever. I now know that my wife and children love me unconditionally. We have all learned great lessons about mind-control and victimization, and as we overcome it, we continue to be way-showers who teach others how they too are subtlely controlled on many levels, and what they can also do to free and control their own minds.

I thank all of you who have called and emailed for your blessings and support. There are a lot of good people out there. The details that I have shared are only the tip of the iceberg. It is my intention to learn from the experience, not dwell on it, and move on. I have a lot of work to do, and I am focusing on rebuilding my life in an even stronger way. Life is indeed sometimes stranger than fiction.

I am sure that because she failed her mission with me, she herself has become a target. The only way she can redeem herself to the Illuminati is to hand them her next victim. She fully intends to take over a major international conference based in Colorado. The founder of that conference is himself a Mason, so perhaps he is in on the plan. He did not stop her from coming to conferences after I warned him about her. He did say that he knew she lied about her age, and thought she was closer to sixty.

The other targets are themselves game-players. All have been duly warned. Now the game will be played out. I learned valuable lessons from this event. In that way, Rosie 2 became my greatest teacher. Johannes loved her, but she was a "thing" to him. Those old feelings were played upon by the master game-players. The time has finally come to cut Rosie 2 from the twisted vine on which she grows. That flower lost its fragrance long ago.

---

[1] I believe Dean was murdered by Rosie 2 in August 2001.

25

SWISS KEYS

Sitting in a pension called "Paulus Akademie" in the Witikon section of Zurich, high in the hills overlooking the city, I reflected upon my first overseas trip since the events of Rosie 2. The Akademie is a Jesuit-run establishment. The rooms are spartan and excruciatingly clean. There are no phones, no radio, no television, no noise. All I heard was the rain falling on the small balcony outside my room. I was totally alone.

This was a difficult trip, cleaning up from the Rosie 2 episode, and righting some of the havoc perpetuated by her on the last visit. The damage was evident. I had half the seminar attendance as usual. The group that sponsored me, Vision 3000, was fighting amongst themselves for control. I did my best to remain neutral, as after all, this was Switzerland.

I had just returned from a rainy evening out with some of the seminar participants and my Swiss sponsors. We were out ringing church bells and chimes from the tower of an old Lutheran church near the Bahnhofstrasse—Zurich's version of New York City's 5th Avenue. Every Saturday evening, church bells and chimes are rung downtown in a certain order, one church after another. One of my sponsors is responsible to ring the bells of one of the churches. Together, we ascended the ancient wooden stairway to the top. I saw a male ghost, all dressed in black hovering near one of the walls as the bells sounded.

After we left the church, the sponsor took us through the rain on a walking tour of the old city, stopping by each of the churches as its bells were rung. The cobblestone streets and hilly terrain threw me back to a time when I walked the same location wearing long black garb with black leather boots. I was a Spanish priest, and stayed here frequently. The images stopped as quickly as they started when we turned an ancient corner to face the Zurich River. I was so tired. I had not slept in two days, and had stood for over eight hours during my seminar, plus three the previous night at that lecture.

I also reflected on my flight over to Zurich. I wore my star tetrahedron pendant, and as I took my seat in the coach section, a flight attendant asked me about it. Always cautious with strangers, I explained that it had to do with sacred geometry. She said that she was a Reiki practitioner who was trying to cure her dying sister of cancer. I invited her to attend the Zurich seminar, which was on healing techniques.

Because she was to be there for only a few hours, she asked to speak to me privately during the flight. My seatmate, who happened to be a well-known Swiss musician, overheard our conversation. He asked me to help a friend with a bipolar problem. Then he mentioned that he had put the Book of Revelation to music. I found this synchronistic, because I translated the Book of Revelation in my book, *As Ye Sow,* (out of print) based on color and archetype.

After dinner, the flight attendant called me to the back of the plane to discuss her sister. I wrote down ideas and techniques for her. I also invited her to attend my upcoming seminar in Vermont, her home state. She was so overwhelmed that she burst out crying. I felt my strength to help others return, and thanked God for this journey. Even if it were not financially successful, at least I had helped someone.

I returned to my seat to try to sleep. Within minutes, the flight attendant was in the aisle, motioning me to come with her. She took me to a small corridor, closing the curtain behind us. Then, she whispered, "I could lose my job for this, but because I'm the senior team member, I have the rest of the crew on my side. I'm moving you to Business Class because you are feeling so ill and need more room."

I was stunned! The last two trips I had taken, I was amazingly bumped up to Business Class by the airline for being such a "good customer." I had hoped it would happen again because once anyone flies this way, they never want to fly coach again. God helped me again because I helped this stranger.

The flight attendants treated me like royalty the rest of the way. I practically had the entire Business Class section to myself. Several flight attendants constantly tended to me — I was almost embarrassed!

Before we landed, another older flight attendant handed me a large airline bag, saying, "Here is a box of chocolates for your wife. Thank you so much for helping the senior flight attendant."

Again, I was speechless. To me, what I did was a matter of course. I thought nothing of it except to be grateful to be of service. To these wonderful people, I had done something that touched their hearts, and I in turn, was touched by their expression of gratitude.

My mind returned back to my hotel, Paulus Akademie, named after St. Paul the Apostle. Long ago, I was told by both my main Montauk deprogrammer and a well-known UFO researcher, that I have the DNA of St. Paul within me. I was always fascinated by his lifetime, including his corresponding wanderlust, eye difficulties, and ability to write. I studied everything I could about his lifetime and journeys. I saw myself picking up where he left off, but with a different, more unadulterated version of the message. Even his imprisonment reminded me of myself. His tutoring of St. Peter was synchronistic to my tutoring of my cubicle mate, Peter, who helped me with two of my books.

Being in this quiet place away from home made me contemplate that lifetime. I thought of being sent through time from Montauk with orders to kill the Christ and get a vial of His blood. Because I could not carry out the orders, I was sent again while He was on the cross. This time, I removed the blood from His foot, then brought it to Mars for cloning.[1]

Here alone, I realized how much I missed Janet and my children. I wished they were here with me. Yet, I valued the alone time and ability to do quiet work. I knew that great changes would happen soon in my life after this trip. Much of the garbage was purged out of me. I needed to be in this " neutral" place in this "neutral" country to naturally open my mind-pattern and DNA in order to complete what I came to do in this lifetime.

I also realized that it is because of Janet, with her Magdalene and Cherokee energies, that I am able to be who I truly am, without fear or self-doubt. How do you repay a person for this? I am not sure, but I will spend the rest of my mortal life figuring this out.

---

[1] Refer to *Montauk: The Alien Connection (Sky Books, 1998)*.

26

BOY FROM BRAZIL

I have always had an affinity with Brazil. So, when my Chicago sponsor asked to join his group on a journey to Central Brazil to observe a man called, Joao de Deus, or, John Of God, I immediately agreed. This peasant-like person, whose family owns vast semi-precious stone mines, supposedly channels thirty-two different entities who diagnose illnesses and perform medical procedures through him. I previewed his "surgeries" on a video, and had serious doubts about his authenticity. High-level beings do not need, or want, to possess the bodies of others to do their work on the Earth plane.

I found out that it takes two days to get a Brazilian visa that is good for five years, plus there is a cost for it. I braved the snow flurries in October 2000 and crowded train ride with Janet and my two youngest children to venture into New York City where I had to stand in a long line at the Brazilian Consulate. That was to be the easiest part of my adventure.

First, I flew to Atlanta, then transferred to a flight to South America. That flight went first to Caracas, which reminded me of a cross between Los Angeles, New York City, and San Juan. Then we flew over the area of Venezuela that borders Brazil. This plateau region is isolated and remote, and slightly larger than New York State. Here, there are real, living dinosaurs that still exist in their own world. Time stands still in this location. The same is true for remote parts of Central Congo in Africa, where natives and explorers claim that dinosaur creatures still roam.

I looked down at the mighty Amazon Basin. The thick foliage and twisting rivers seemed foreboding, and the air looked thick with humidity and haze. I knew that prehistoric Earth, and possibly Lemuria, looked like that. My flight to Rio de Janeiro and Sao Paolo was long but comfortable. I will always be grateful to Delta Airlines for their hospitality and great service.

I disembarked at the Sao Paolo airport. This sprawling city of almost 20 million people is the second largest in the world, after Mexico City. Crime here is rampant. People kill for a pair of sneakers. The wealthy barricade themselves behind electric fences with armed guards. Groups of homeless children wander about in search of money and food. Police often shoot to kill in an effort to rid the city of its bad reputation. Large numbers of these children disappear every year. I am sure that many of them are used in experimentation and ritual since they would not be missed. Sao Paolo is the perfect source of material for the Illuminati.

At this airport, there are not enough gates to accommodate the many flights to the vast interior and coast of the country. I was confused and anxious as I located the correct plane to Brasilia. At my gate, there were also flights to Natal, Recife, and San Salvador. The announcements were poor and only in Portuguese, which is a difficult language to audibly understand, even when one speaks other romance languages.

We arrived in Brasilia one-half hour late. I rushed to the designated location to meet my hosts and the bus to Abidiania. I arrived at the meeting spot at 11:56am. I later found out that they left at 11:55am after an hour wait. I waited for another hour, hoping to hear an announcement or English-speaking voice. It was the rainy season, and I was hot and sticky. No one that I spoke with ever heard of Joao de Deus, or the small town of Abidiania. I called home several times to check for any messages the group might have left.

Finally, after three hours of waiting, I decided to look for a local hotel for the night. I asked God for a sign. Just then, a short, dark-skinned native Indian woman walked up to me and asked me a question in Portuguese about the buses. I responded in Spanish, saying I was a foreigner and did not speak Portuguese. I added that I was lost. She told me her name was Maria, and that she was from a Brazilian tribe that lived near the Bolivian border.

Maria literally took me by the hand to find the information booth, which was quite far away. There, we found a note left by my sponsor telling me to find the bus depot, and take a bus to the town, about three hours from Brasilia. Next, Maria took me to an airport bus, and together we rode downtown to the bus station. On the way, she gave me a tour of the city, telling me about the various buildings and sights. Curiously, Maria, the driver, and I were the only bus occupants on the entire trip.

After showing me the little shops at the depot, Maria ordered us a delicious fruit drink and a chicken-filled pastry from a typical native food stand. Then, she took me to buy my ticket, and waited with me by the bus stop. When the bus arrived, she told the driver where I was going and told him to inform me where to get off. After thanking Maria profusely, we exchanged business cards. This angel came out of nowhere to rescue me from confusion and worry. I certainly believe in Angels!

The bus ride was difficult through heavy rain and slow traffic. The roads were winding and hilly. We passed many accidents and even saw a dead body on the road where a huge truck had overturned. It seemed to take forever. I fought to stay awake because I did not want to miss the stop.

Three hours after leaving Brasilia, I finally arrived in a sleepy, dirt road village. The driver turned to me, pointing his finger down a deserted street. I kept thinking that all I wanted was a shower and bed. The pouring rain soaked me to the bone in about twenty seconds. Chickens, skinny dogs, and old horses scampered in the street. It was getting dark, and all the buildings were closed up without a soul around.

Since I was supposed to be arriving in Abidiania with my sponsor, I did not have the address of my hotel. In my mind, I was deciding whether I should hug him or kill him! After wandering around for about thirty minutes, I heard a thick Irish brogue from a nearby building. That was English enough for me! The kind youth told me that a group of Americans from Chicago had recently arrived, and he took me to their posada. They were worried about me, and glad to see my face. All I cared about at that point was a shower, but of course, the water was not working!

During my few days in Abidiania , I constantly had an uneasy feeling like I should not even be there. Janet did not want me to go in the first place. I did meet many interesting people and new clients, but something was not right.

Joao works in a large complex. When I first viewed Joao, he seemed rather strange. His eyes appeared glassed-over and detached; not a very spiritual appearance. In fact, he was rather unkempt. He sees people only three days per week. Much of the time, the compound is packed. His services are free, but he assigns people to crystal baths, herbs, and waterfall treatments, for which there are charges. When a person receives surgery, either psychic or physical, that person must take a taxi back to his/her posada. The cabs form a long line outside the compound, waiting for these people. I am sure that Joao receives some monetary compensation from them. Without him, the town would not exist.

Before seeing Joao, his assistants speak to the crowd from a raised platform stage, riling the people up into a spiritual frenzy with singing, praying, and praises to Joao. This reminded me of a Nazi rally, or even a

Tony Robbins seminar. The lead speaker is of German descent, and for some odd reason, asked me to help him get into Canada.

Joao's primary assistant is a small man named Sebastian who reminded me of "Tattoo," from the 1970s *Fantasy Island* television show. Sebastian oversaw a "room of horrors," that contained body parts, tumors, and other disgusting objects removed by Joao over the years. To me, it seemed more Illuminati than Godly to keep such a room.

While standing in the main foyer of the healing building, I felt a radiating energy coming up from underground. I mentioned this to someone, and was then informed that a large crystal was buried under the floor. I thought that strange. Why would they want to amplify something from underground?

During the three days I visited the compound, I saw Joao perform eye scrapings and abdominal surgery on people who stood on the stage. He used an old, dirty knife, and did not clean it between operations. Before I left on this trip, a man from Vermont called to tell me that when his eyes were scraped the pain was so severe that he almost fell to the floor. He wanted my help to heal the damage.

People in the audience, and even in the posadas, suddenly claimed that Joao's "entities" were talking to them. There was some kind of hysteria occurring amongst the visitors. This did not appear to be a positive thing. Possession and fainting are signs of demonic events, not high-level spiritual beings. I saw absolutely no one healed in any way.

Ultimately, a person must heal themselves. I think that anyone experiencing a healing there believed so strongly that something would happen that they create it themselves. A mind-pattern of low self-worth prevents people from taking responsibility for the healings, so they credit Joao.

One morning while walking to the compound, we saw Joao whiz by in a new American sports coupe smoking a cigarette. That was interesting! This man who claims not to be able to read or write was able to get a driver's license and buy an expensive car. I was later told that several nights per week he goes into the larger city of Anapolis where he spends time with women, smoking, dancing, and drinking. Perhaps his name should be John of Scam.

Another gentleman told me that the assistant followed him to the men's room and watched him when he used the facilities. The overall feeling was one of strict adherence to compound rules. Anyone acting outside these rules is ridiculed. There was a "Jim Jones," or cult, sense to the place. I do believe that Joao allows his body to be used, but to me he usually appears as though he is Reptilian possessed.

While there, I met the half brother of a well-known actress from the 1960s. He was staying in the same Posada with me. Interestingly, he arrived on the same day as I did, and was flying back on the same day. He offered me to share his taxi and I accepted.

He claimed to be a good friend of Dack Rambo's. Readers of my *Montauk: The Alien Connection* book will remember that I worked with Dack on healing AIDS. It was interesting to talk to him. We drove back to Brasilia together, and flew back to Sao Paolo. It was good to not have to travel alone.

While I waited for my flight to the states, I noticed a man sitting across from me. Thinking he looked familiar, I finally identified him as the husband of the actress who accompanied George and myself to the Montauk Base and Maine! He was the star of a popular television drama series. What was he doing here?

Then, while standing in the check-in line, I was approached by a uniformed man, who asked me if I had only carry on luggage. When I answered in the affirmative, he told me to please follow him. My heart sank. Why did he single me out from everyone else in the line?

I followed him across the airport terminal to an unmarked counter. We were the only ones there. Taking my tickets, he left the counter. Standing there alone, I began to worry. Finally, he returned with boarding passes for both return flights, telling me that most passengers are unaware of this service. He added that the next time I leave Sao Paolo, I should return to this very counter. I walked away, then watched from a distance. The uniformed man left the area. Not a single other person, passenger or otherwise, went to that counter.

I was so happy to return home to a cool, bugless environment. I have no desire to ever return to Brazil. When I looked for Maria's card so that I could email her a thank you, it was gone! I turned everything inside out. I knew I had it when I left Brazil because I checked my luggage compartment where I put it. How could it disappear? If you are out there, Maria, please let me know. Or were you really an Angel?! Perhaps there was another reason I had to travel to a city named after St. Paul.

27

FUTURE ILLUMINATI PLANS

After so many thousands of years, the Reptilian plans for total control are almost accomplished. In essence, it is done. The one major factor that remains is for the Earth's population to openly know it. This is currently in motion with the illegal election of George W. Bush to the presidency. He was filmed on CNN shortly after the botched Florida court voted in his favor "joking" about being a dictator. This is no joke!

One major goal that remains to occur is the plan to reduce the status of the United States to that of a typical third world nation. The United States has grown too big for Illuminati plans. They cannot allow a superpower populated with self-righteous, arrogant millions to continue to exist. They intend to deflate the power of its citizenry.

In the 1850s, the Illuminati set the date 2000 as their target goal for total global domination. They are behind schedule due to various factors, and have revised their goal to be achieved between 2003 and 2010. The beginning of that period, 2003, seems to be a critical time period.

In 1996-97, the Hale Bopp comet passing the Earth was in the news. There were reports of an object trailing the comet; a huge spaceship the size of the Moon. There was even a cult in San Diego that killed themselves, expecting their consciousnesses to awaken on board that ship. After that mass murder/suicide, an Illuminati ritual tradition, anyone who believed in the trailing object was severely ridiculed. That was the purpose of those deaths – to discredit legitimate information.

The fact is that a black, moon-sized object was deposited behind the dark side of the Moon, which is itself a ship. In this black object are tens of millions of pure Reptilians from the Draco star system. They are here as part of the invasion agenda that began hundreds of thousands of years earlier. The problem is that the original colony, brought on the original Moon/ship, has not accomplished their goal of global domination. In addition, the original colony developed a hybrid Reptilian subculture, known as the Illuminati, that was not part of the original plan.

The Illuminati are in trouble, and they know it. They are preparing to pacify "Mommy/Daddy" Draco before any violence occurs against the Illuminati themselves. This is why the pure Reptilians under the Earth are coming to the surface, and fires are being set in those areas to keep people away. The object behind the Moon, as it comes closer, is causing windstorms, volcanic eruptions, earthquakes, and weather anomalies all over the Earth.

The major Illuminati families are no longer hiding their true identities. Queen Elizabeth was photographed wringing the neck of a pheasant in ceremony style. Her grandson, William, was photographed giving the "Devil's Salute." Eventually shapeshifting will become public, much the same as their ancestors in Ancient Lemuria.

The monetary system is changing to a global currency. Several countries already use or accept the United States dollar bill as their own currency, including Panama, Ecuador, Costa Rica, Mexico, Israel, the Philippines, and all of the Caribbean except Cuba. Argentina has a one peso for one-dollar exchange rate. For the most part, the new European currency, the Euro, is at a one to one exchange. Eventually this one global currency, controlled from a single source, will be exchanged for a credit system. No more cash. This is why credit cards have been hoisted upon the public for the last thirty years.

An artificial, copper-based blood is now being manufactured for future use. When this blood is injected into the body, it totally replicates itself, replacing the original blood. The goal is for everyone to have this same blood type. This is why so many people are finding it difficult to access their own blood types when they ask their doctors for it.

All food will be genetically altered. The farming of any original DNA structures will be prohibited. Radionic waves will prevent any secret original crops or animals from being harvested. They simply will not grow.

Cloning will become common place. The first human clone in the United States was created in 1967 at Massachusetts Institute of Technology (M.I.T.) in Massachusetts. The Germans actually perfected cloning in 1927. Right now, on the Moon are over 40,000 cloned Aryan-style soldiers. There are almost 15,000 such clone copies at the Mars underground locations. The Reptilians find these Aryan genetics desirable and more controllable. Eventually, there will be vast warehouses filled with cloned, headless human bodies whose sole purpose is to provide organs and limbs for the population.

Listed below are the planned scenarios of destruction for the United States, followed by the planned events leading to total Illuminati global domination.

THE UNITED STATES
2001 – 2003

• Elimination of fuel reserves.
• Creation of severe weather patterns designed to consume the remaining fuel.
• Utilities will be unable to cope with the demand.
• Regional natural disasters so large that local civil authorities are unable to handle them.
• Rioting and chaos in major US cities.
• Polarization of minorities creating a call from the minorities for a need for segregation.
• Martial law declared to restore order.
• Economic/stock market collapse as a result of the disasters, lack of utilities, and planned chaos.
• President will enact Executive Orders that in effect, will rescind the Constitution and civil rights.
• The United Nations will be called in to restore order. This comes with waves of Chinese, Russian, and German troops already stationed around the United States borders.
• Dissidents will be shipped for re-education to huge concentration camps already in place in the United States and Canada.
• The United Nations declares that the US is too large to be administered as is, and will order it to be split into two districts; Eastern and Western.
• The Eastern district capital will be Atlanta. The Western district capital will be Denver. This is why government offices and international super-airports were built in these two cities.
• Washington D.C. will become an Illuminati cultural site and possibly even a religious center for them.
• New York City will be declared the United Nations capital city for the Earth and given special status. This is why New York State is called the "Empire State."
• Undesirables will be eliminated via chemtrails, "mosquito spraying,"

flu shots, and other inoculations.
- Radicals will simply be executed.
- Programming centers will become standard sites for children to visit - Montauk Point, DisneyWorld/Orlando, Disneyland/Anaheim, Mt. Shasta, Sedona, Santa Fe, Yelm, and Huntsville Space Center.
- All airforce bases will be staging areas.
- National parks will be declared International Sites and come under United Nations jurisdiction.
- All people will be issued identity cards that will contain their DNA.

GLOBAL PLANS[1]
2001 – 2010

- A Middle Eastern war, coupled with a world financial collapse, will center attention to the United Nations as a control factor.
- China and Israel will attack and destroy the Moslem Fundamentalists in Central and Western Asia.
- The Earth will be divided into three major political/economic units - North and South America, including Central America and the Caribbean; Europe, Africa, and the Middle East; and, the Pan-Asia/ Australian region.
- A staged alien invasion will occur, forcing all nations, religions, and cultures to give up separate identities and unite under the United Nations/Illuminati/Global Government. The US dollar already says *Novus Ordo Seclorem*, i.e., *New World Order.* The United States new army slogan was recently changed after decades to, "An Army of One."
- Certain alien group will be introduced as heroes who saved the Earth. This will likely be the group from Sirius A.
- "Peace" will be made with the Reptilians, and the hybrid-Illuminati Reptilians will be touted as the logical leaders since they are a 50/50 genetic mixture, blending the two groups together.
- A New World Religion will be introduced and enforced upon all people. This religion will have the male/female, God/Goddess, as Princess Diana and Emmanuel, hence the Second Coming of Christ.
- A cloned Christ will be sent to Earth from Mars, proclaiming the

New World Order and His New Holy Empire.

• All money and assets will belong to the New Earth Empire. A global credit system will be imposed.

• All Earth citizens will have mandatory identification cards with their DNA imprinted upon them. These will be monitored via satellite.

• Total mind-control will be the rule of the day, with transmissions coming from satellites, amplified by ground towers, cell phones, radio, and television. Children are already programmed by shows like Pokeman, Barney, Teletubbies, Ninja Turtles, and most shows on Cartoon Network and Nickelodeon.

• The Dome of the Rock Mosque will be destroyed and the Temple of Solomon will be rebuilt there. The Ark of the Covenant will be relocated there.

• Blacks will be eliminated from the Earth except for those that have a mixture of genetics with other races, like the Ethiopians, Sudanese, and some United States and Caribbean Blacks.

• Atlantean technology will be revealed and exploited.

• Interplanetary and interdimensional travel will openly be available to select people.

• Jupiter will become a second sun, making this a Binary Star System. This is a result of the String of Pearls Comet (technology) that struck that gas giant in 1994.

• Frozen moons of Saturn, Jupiter, and Neptune will become Earth-like after the new sun shines, and a redistribution of Earth's huge population will begin. At least three billion people will be re-colonized on at least six new "Earths."

• Earth will become the center of a tyrannical Empire that will fan out amongst the stars and universes, continuing the conquer-and-assimilate agenda.

• All people will have a chip placed in their skulls connecting them to a central computer control system.

• The so-called "Indigo Children," a code name for the Illuminati to "Indicate" children with abilities will be confiscated from their parents and trained by the Empire.

Is there any hope? Should people hide in their closets? Should anyone fight back? The answers to these questions are yes, no, and no. Each individual is the hope. There are *no* space brothers waiting to save this population. These are Reptilian leaders from the astral planes who deceive mankind. Even Jesus/Emmanuel was an admitted alien creation. Most human civilizations that exist elsewhere are totalitarian also. This is a necessity because of the constant Reptilian threat.

Each person on Earth must gain control of his/her own minds to find out who and what they truly are within God-Mind. Then, if they teach others to do the same, eventually this will extrapolate to a critical mass that will spill over to the rest of the population. Then there will be no need or possibility for any victim-mentality to exist, and no oppressor will be attracted. Mankind will then be free. This new mind-pattern of the species can even be taught to the Reptilians, and any other race or type of beings. God-Mind allows all. In God-Mind, this solution has already occurred! Everyone must now become aware of it.

[1] This book went to press shortly after the 9-11-2001 attack on the United States. These incidents verify the Global Agends outline in this book. For more detailed information on the terrorist attacks, please visit my website, www.stewartswerdlow.com, which outlines specific plans and rationales. Unfortunately, it is all coming true.

28

REFLECTIONS & OBSERVATIONS

I learned many difficult and valuable lessons over these last decades, with the most intense lessons learned the last two years. As with everyone, just when I thought that I knew my information, my Oversoul, or master mind-pattern, tested me again to see if I could pass the final exam. As with most people, I failed that final exam. People have a tendency to become smug and self-assured, feeling that nothing and no one can touch them. This is what happened to me.

If anyone who was similarly programmed says that he/she is completely and totally deprogrammed, they are not telling the truth. Perhaps lessons are learned, and the mistakes are more easily observed and corrected, but the imprinting remains. A duck is still a duck, even if it is a brilliant duck. Ducks are also targets.

Before Rosie 2 came into my life, I believed that I could never be reprogrammed again. I thought that I had all of the tools and abilities to perceive danger and deception. I was wrong. I am reminded of the famed columnist, Ann Landers, who advised countless of thousands of people on marital situations, while at the same time losing her own spouse. That did not mean that she was less wise, it only means that she was not paying attention to herself.

Healers and counselors attract clients who are going through issues similar to their own. That is a Universal Law. When you pay attention to your client's issues, you are able to find a solution to your own.

I should have realized several years ago that most of my clients had serious control issues that manifested in their marriages and workplaces. Their children did not want to see them and their parents gave them a hard time. Many were cheating on their spouses. Hello! Did I look in the mirror? Sometimes, but then I quickly looked away. A part of me thought that I was above that. Wrong!

Janet and I came to a place where we argued about everything. Rosie 2 constantly told me that I was getting a divorce. Because of the manipulated situation that I was experiencing, I believed her, but was revolted at the same time. I could not tolerate even the thoughts of Janet dating another man, or my children being raised by another man.

Even though at the time, they probably would have been better off that way.

On the few occasions that I was home between trips, my older children grew increasingly aloof. My younger children refused to let me hug or kiss them. That killed me inside, but still I left on the next trip. My work became more important than my home life, which I was influenced to believe did not exist anyway.

Removing a person's home base and security is a primary Illuminati control method to break a person's will. Couples worldwide reported to me that they either had severe problems or were breaking up. Even other counselor/clients reported the same situation in their practices. A depressed population without a family base is not so willing to fight when they are oppressed. They do not feel that they have anything worth fighting for.

My advice to everyone is to fix your personal problems first. Make correcting your mind-pattern a priority in your life. I found out, almost too late, that money and work is meaningless when there is no one there to share it with you.

Feel what you feel. If you are depressed, feel it, look at the physical and mental reasons, then release it. Do not stop until you are successful. You are the *only* one responsible for everything in your life. If you do not accept responsibility, the solution cannot be found.

There are many people out there who will provide agitation for you to live out your chosen mind-patterns. But remember, it takes two; one to provide an influence, and one to accept or reject it. Both parties are equally responsible for their parts.

I reflect a lot on my children. Despite my prolonged absences, they are all turning out exceptionally well. That credit goes to their respective mothers, who did their best under often difficult circumstances. We do not own our children. One day they grow up with a life of their own. We cannot expect to be included in every minute of it. That is a hard lesson for me. When I look at my older children, I still see those adorable, cute little babies and toddlers. I still want to see them every night and weekend. But this changed. I cannot put the burden of my happiness on them. They have a right to their friends and lifestyles. I am grateful that they do not miss me when I am gone. When I do see them now, it is wonderful and we enjoy each other's company.

A person must be happy within him/herself. No other being can make you happy if you are not happy already. Once you find happiness within, then it becomes a matter of deciding with whom you wish to share your happiness. For me, my rare alone time is one of my greatest pleasures. One cannot be of service to others if one has nothing left to give.

This world, in fact the sum total of physical reality, is an error in God-Mind thinking. That alone appears to be a blasphemous statement! The sum of all physical realities combined is a small blip within God-Mind that is already resolved. We simply have not realized that yet.

Physical reality exists only because of our refusal to take responsibility for our mind-patterns. Physical reality provides an environment where our thoughts are instantly externalized. That is the bottom line explanation of why we are here. This also explains why so many of us feel like we do not belong here. But that does not mean that it is correct to hate or disavow our physicality. On the contrary, we must be grateful and thankful to the God-Mind for allowing this so that we may learn our lessons. The thought behind all of this is as beautiful as a tree or flower. We easily see what serves or hurts us when we pay attention.

People who attend my lectures on the Illuminati and Montauk Project sometimes comment on its negativity, saying that I am instilling fear in the audience. I only speak the truth. I cannot instill in a person something that is not already there. My lectures do not put it there. If what I say makes a person angry, afraid, or upset, then there are issues inside that person that he/she needs to address.

I share what I know so that people will not run blindfolded toward a cliff. With my words, I take off the blindfold so that people can see what is out there. I want people to understand why they are running toward a cliff wearing a blindfold, and I hope and pray that they will choose not to jump over the cliff.

Every person can make a difference in the world. Everyone is here for a specific reason. There are no accidents. There is no waste. Our biggest enemies are really our greatest teachers. Without them, we would not know our fears. You become what you fear and hate. That is how you know it, and then transmute it.

Sometimes people come up to me after a lecture to say that love can change everything. Love is *not* enough. Love is simply an energy like all other energies in the God-Mind.

Love has both positive and negative qualities, depending upon how you choose to use it. I can love you unconditionally, or I can love you to death. I can take a pen and write beautiful poetry, or I can jam it in your eye. The energy of the pen has not changed. A pen is still a pen.

By the time I finish writing this book, until the time you read it, many things will have occurred in the world. I hope that the information contained herein helps you to better understand world events. With that understanding, perhaps many things will be prevented from happening in this time line. This is really up to each one of you, including me.

Everything that you ever need is already inside of you. Be aware of this, and apply it. Always move forward, never giving up.

The purpose of this book is to impart the true history of who and what you are. Through my own personal experiences, I have shown you how this can be applied to a human life.

Let each one of us realize our connection to the species mind-pattern, and in turn, its connection to the God-Mind. Then let us consciously remove all the victim mentality, abusive thoughts, low self-worth, need for insulation, and feelings of lack. Let us co-create a new species mind-pattern that will propel us to the highest levels of awareness.

We can create heaven on Earth right now. We are the only ones stopping ourselves. There is a new world coming. Which one will it be?

APPENDICES

ALIEN GROUPS

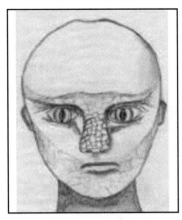

Abbennakki

In the Reptilian races there was a civilization of extremely brilliant beings who took it upon themselves to correct and upgrade DNA programming wherever they could. Their representatives at the meeting on Hatona refused to accept the conditions for Project Earth as proposed by the Council. Instead, they sent instructions to their emissaries, the Abbennakki, to upgrade the DNA on Earth by manipulating the primate population. The Abbennakki believed that all life forms should be upgraded to light capacity, including insect, animal, and even plant life. The Abbennakki are believed to be responsible for many of the intelligent life forms that appear in non-humanoid form such as the Butterfly, Praying Mantis, etc.

The Abbennakki live on a mechanized world called Marduk, and sometimes Niburu, a hollowed-out planet programmed for galactic orbit. Such worlds exist in many nearby galaxies, each sent from their creators in the Andromeda Galaxy with a wide, preprogrammed orbit. Woe unto any world, or object in its path, i.e., the fifth world in this solar system. NASA has noted such a planet and reported it to the press. It is due back in this vicinity in 2003.

Marduk passes the Earth once every 12,000 years. When it gets within a reasonable distance, the Abbennakki visit the target world for a few centuries to do their work. As Marduk starts to speed away, the Abbennakki take off from the target world until the next pass.

Between visitations the Abbennakki employ a group of small beings called the "Bear" who watch and monitor the target planets. Little is known about this group except that their brains are mechanically controlled and programmed, and they follow explicit orders from Marduk.

The Atlans mixed bear genetics with human to create the Bigfoot/ Yeti creatures.

Aldebaran

These beings are the typical Aryan-type with blonde hair and blue eyes. Occasionally, there are people with light or medium brown hair and hazel eyes. This group was responsible for the creation and manipulation of the Germanic Tribes, and the Scandinavian peoples, particularly the Vikings. They are extremely focused on getting the Lyraen civilization recreated under their auspices. People sometimes confuse them with the "Nordics" who are much taller and more arrogant. The Aldebaranians are approximately six feet tall with a slender to medium build. They are very technological, non-emotional, no-nonsense types. The "Nordics" tampered with the Viking culture unsuccessfully, but did leave their more massive genetics.

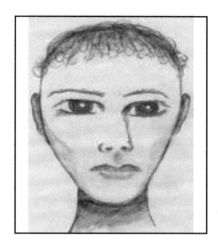

Antaries

Extremely belligerent and aggressive, these beings keep to themselves, have strange customs and practices, and wear skin-tight dark uniforms. Their DNA has been traced tot he Turks, Greeks, and European Spaniards. Females have never been observed with them, and it is believed that they are a homosexual society that uses females only for procreation purposes. It is believed that a matriarchal group is actually a power source behind them. Very few are able to infiltrate the deepest layers of their society.

Officially, they are only here to observe, but there are reports of abductions by this group in the United States, parts of Southern Europe, and Asia Minor. They are olive-skinned with black hair and eyes, slender, and have completely human-like anatomy. They are approximately five and one-half to six feet tall.

Arcturus

These extremely spiritual beings have an elementary form of space travel, i.e., more advanced than Earth, but not as high-tech as the Sirians. They are ruled by a priestly class that wears white robes. Their pure society lives without violence, war, disease, poverty, or pollution on their planet.

When one of their spacecraft crashed on the Italian Peninsula during the time of the Greek civilization, they came to Earth by accident. About one-thousand years later another craft came to look for them. Those beings stayed to help develop the original Roman Empire.

During the last 2000 years their culture has developed a significant space technology. They are helping to salvage some humans on specially prepared planets arranged for them by the Galactic Federation and other groups. The Arcturians are known for their peaceful ways and non-interference in the affairs of others. Many beings go to their star system to study divine concepts or to mediate conflicts.

Atlans (Lyraens)

This culture experienced a "refugee syndrome." They were originally Lyraens who fled to the Pleiades during the civil wars. After a millennium, disagreements with the High Lyraen Council resulted in the establishment of many colonies elsewhere in the galaxy—one of which became Atlantis.

A blonde-haired, blue-eyed race with heavily developed pineal glands, their genetics can be traced to North American Indian groups, ancient Egypt, Persia, and the Indians of Northern Brazil.

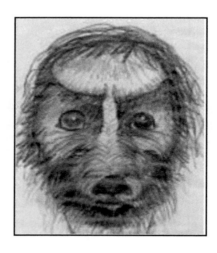

Bear

The Bear have been seen mainly in Africa, the Caribbean, and parts of the United States, basically because the Abbennakki creations on Earth were the Black Race. The Abbennakki create higher life forms from lower ones which explains why many African tribes worship various animals as intelligent, god-like beings. The Bear are usually small and powerful, but some are larger than humans.

The United States government, in an effort to prevent the Abbennakki from returning to collect their creations and to eliminate the Black Race from the Earth, released the AIDS virus into the Black African and Haitian populations, hoping that this information would be transmitted to Marduk, preventing any landings by them on this planet.

Butterfly

A completely silent entity, the Butterfly always hovers, touching the ground or walls only when in a sleep state. They are mostly non-physical, and are approximately eight feet tall.

Draco

Created by an ET group, the creators traveled back in time and space with genetic material to support the disintegration of the Lyraen civilization. With seven different types of Draco races, the leader group is a seven to eight foot tall winged reptilian-type creature. Above is pictured a warrior used to conquer and occupy a planet. The slender four to five foot Draco similar to a lizard performs menial tasks and aids in abductions.

Harsh, warlike beings who feel little emotion, the Draco have no regard for culture or other beings. Most Draco are androgynous and reproduce by parthenogenesis, or cloning. One special group that is completely male creates hybrid races that conquer others.

The Earth's Moon is a Draco planetoid placed in orbit aeons ago during the time of the Lemurian colonization. With the intention to divide and conquer, they are known to be brutal, as with Rigel by boiling oceans, scorching landmasses, etc. The Draco have vast underground bases on Earth and colonies on Venus.

A second Moon has been stationed over the Earth. It arrive behind the Hale-Bopp Comet in 1997. These are pure Reptilians. The hybrids, Illuminati, are in control of the Earth.

Extraterrestrial Biological Entity (EBE)

These aliens were given their name by the United States Government. They appear to be plant material rather than biological, and absorb energy directly from the sun. They are approximately three feet tall.

Pleiadians

Also known as the Nordics, or tall blondes, these beings are from the seven star Pleiadian system that contains 15 inhabited planets, they were refugees from the Lyraen civilization. After the United States government realized in 1959 that the Rigelians had deceived them, the Pleiadians were invited to fill the technological gap. However, these beings orchestrated Hitler's attempt to purify the human race, subverted the Buddhist religion, have an extensive underground base in Tibet, and beam Extremely Low Frequency (ELF) to various groups of humans who "channel" benevolent "space brothers" from the Pleiades. These beings are generally six to seven feet tall.

The Pleiadians are under a Supreme Council headed by non-physical beings appearing as robed, white figures. One group of Pleiadians, known as the Atlans, colonized Atlantis. There is a smaller blue-skinned group that works with the Pleiadians. The shorter dark-haired Pleiadians are the ones who are in contact with Billy Meier in Switzerland and are benevolent beings. In all, there are sixteen different Pleiadian groups amongst the seven stars of that system.

Praying Mantis

An extremely benevolent creature. The Praying Mantis emits a constant, loud, chirping and clicking sound that is disturbing to humans. They are approximately seven to eight feet tall and four to five feet long.

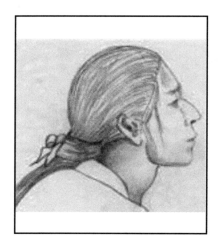

Procyon

These stately beings have bronze skin, golden-brown eyes, and golden-bronze hair. They are extremely spiritual, but without advanced technology, they need to be transported by others – usually via an interstellar transport beam developed by ETs.

They are in charge of upgrading the Draco remnants from Lemuria by mixing their DNA with them. In this way, they developed the cultures of Central and South America before departing this planet. They further mixed Atlantean DNA with some of the groups in the Yucatan and Peruvian Andes. They were ferried back and forth during the last stages of this experiment by a group within the Galactic Federation. They are approximately seven feet tall.

Rigel

This group signed an agreement with the United States government in 1954 exchanging their technology and scientific information in return for the United States allowing them to abduct, but not injure, United States citizens. Physically and genetically weak due to the wars that ravaged their planet during the Lyraen Civil War and the subsequent Draco invasion of their star system, they work for the Draco by scouting planets on the invasion route to prepare them for capture.

They have a military-type culture with a definite hierarchy, especially where the Zeta Reticuli I and II greys are concerned, and the ability to transfer souls between bodies. Higher officials often bring "spare" bodies with them as well as "dolls" of themselves as a symbol that they shake at subordinates in the hierarchy to show superiority. They rarely abduct, but are often seen overseeing underground bases and experiments. Generally exhibiting a nasty demeanor and showing little expression except anger, they are the leaders of the Orion Confederation. They are approximately five feet tall.

Sirius A

These tall and slender beings wear long blue and white robes. When they extend their arms straight out to the side, their bodies form an "ankh," which is their symbol. They are merchants of the universe, selling and trading technology and information in exchange for exclusive trade routes and special considerations. They never provide technology that might be used against them. They were created by the Ohaluans, and have lost their true purpose.

They strongly influenced the ancient Egyptian and Hebrew civilizations, and now have an agreement with the Israeli government. They perform genetic experiments, and created the Vegans as their assistants. The Sirians made the Crystal Skull, keeping its reciprocal safeguarded on their home planet, Khoom. They are seven to eight feet tall.

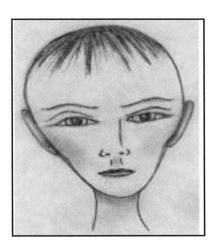

Sirius B

Known throughout the galaxy as "the philosophers," they are the group that influenced Lao Tzu, Confucius, and the original Buddhism. Relying on the Pleiadians and Sirian A's for transportation, they generally do not travel on their own. They store information on long, rough crystal rods that slip into simple computers. They live on a jungle/swamp-like planet, usually as hermits in cave-type hollows or underground, and live for an extremely long time. Most have no known family relationships. Beings from all over the universe visit individual teachers to study and bring information back to their home planets. They are only three and one-half to four feet tall, and very squat.

Tau Ceti

These human-like beings are the archenemies of the grey races, vowing to destroy them wherever they find them in the universe. Long ago, the Rigelians tried to prepare the Tau Ceti system for invasion. To create a grey race with Tau Ceti genetics, their main targets were kidnapped children who were killed for their cells and hormones. The Tau Cetians drove the greys off their world before their race was decimated.

Following the greys to this planet, they signed an agreement during the 1950s with the Soviet Union in exchange for bases and atmospheric freedom to travel. Their goals were to help the USSR retain global domination (Slavs have Tau Ceti genetics), destroy the greys, and then make a deal with the invasion force. It is believed that the Russians recently reneged on this agreement by giving a similar agreement to the Draco advance guard and throwing out the Tau Cetians.

Tau Ceti retains large colonies in the Epsilon Eradanus star system. They have dense bodies due to the atmosphere and gravity on their home world. They are approximately five and one-half feet tall.

Vegans

This grey race was created from the genetics of Sirius A, and are a standard feature on Sirian ships. They perform all the labor, experiments, and menial tasks for their masters. They have also been seen on the ships of the Zeta Reticuli I ships acting as commanders. The Vegans are highly intelligent and physically strong. Because they were similarly created, the Zeta Reticuli I and II greys are willing to be led by them on certain missions, such as abducting humans and collecting mineral samples. Vegans generally have a friendly personality, are gentle but matter-of-fact, and are said to have two hearts. They are approximately seven to eight feet tall.

Zeta Reticuli I

These grey aliens were created by the Rigelians to monitor humans on Earth. They are a mixture of human and Rigelian genetics. Similar to a human fetus, they have four fingers and cloven feet. Famous for abducting humans for hormonal fluids and genetic experiments, they have a group mind and hive-like behavior. Their basic emotions are anger, confusion, fear, and surprise.

Given a barren home world in the Zeta Reticuli I star system, they asked for and received asylum on Earth by the United States government. The Rigelians are angry at them. They have also angered the United States government by lying to them. Now a divided group, they have pragmatic alliances.

Due to their genetic/hormonal deficiencies, they are rapidly dying out. By abducting others they are trying to create a hybrid prototype to save themselves and their culture.

They are approximately four feet tall.

Zeta Reticuli II

These greys are a genetically created member of the Reptilian service ranks. They are completely mind-controlled, and hooked up to a central intelligence, i.e., computer. They act in unison with a group mind. They are "mindless" helpers of the Zeta Reticuli I. Often seen during abduction experiences, they behave in a childlike manner. With three fingers on each hand, and feet without toes or features, they are extremely thin and delicate, appearing to be gentle. Although they have been given a world that orbits Zeta Reticuli II, they have no culture or language of their own. They are approximately three feet tall.

Milky Way Galaxy
Flowchart of Genealogy & History

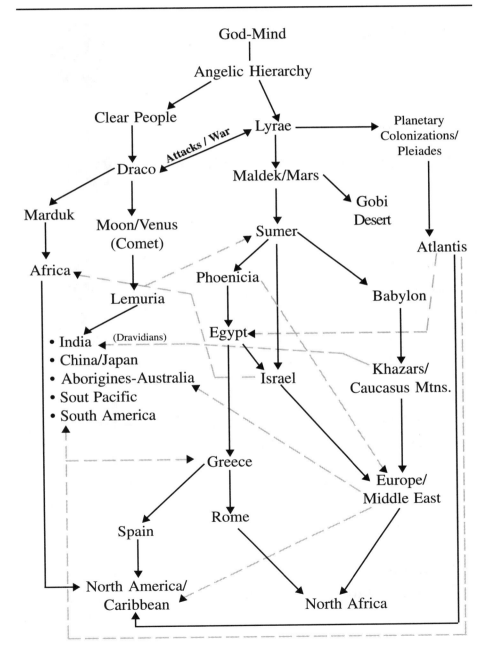

Reptilian Androgyny
Gods / Goddesses ⟶ Earthly Symbols

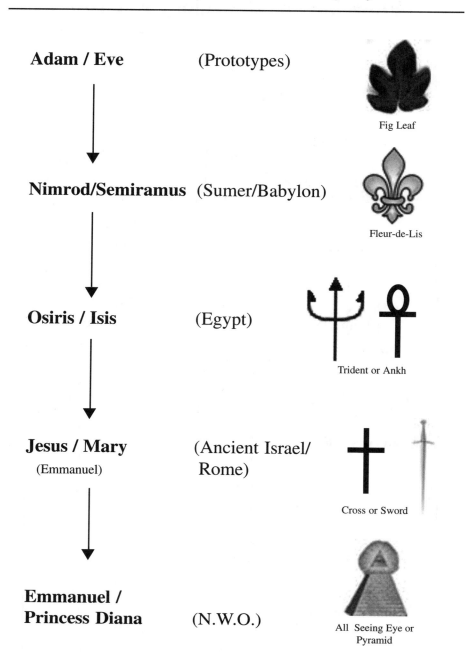

Adam / Eve   (Prototypes)

Fig Leaf

Nimrod/Semiramus   (Sumer/Babylon)

Fleur-de-Lis

Osiris / Isis   (Egypt)

Trident or Ankh

Jesus / Mary   (Ancient Israel/
(Emmanuel)   Rome)

Cross or Sword

**Emmanuel /
Princess Diana**   (N.W.O.)

All Seeing Eye or
Pyramid

Mixture Of Lineages

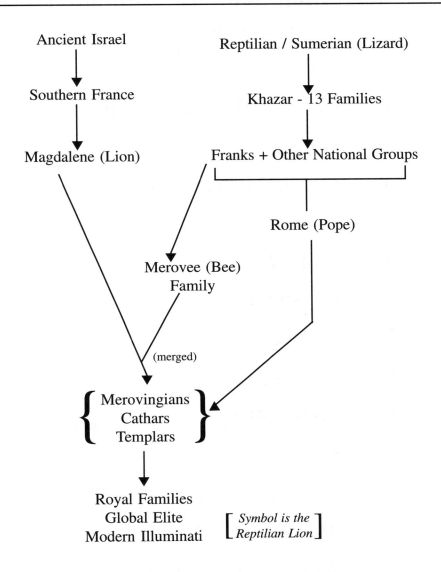

Ancient Israel

Reptilian / Sumerian (Lizard)

Southern France

Khazar - 13 Families

Magdalene (Lion)

Franks + Other National Groups

Rome (Pope)

Merovee (Bee)
Family

(merged)

{ Merovingians
Cathars
Templars }

Royal Families
Global Elite
Modern Illuminati

[Symbol is the
Reptilian Lion]

Numerological Influences:

13 - Families • Colonies • Zodiac • Councils
33 - Parallel • Orders • Degrees
42 - Parallel • Higher Degrees

13 Ruling Families - Illuminati
(Shapeshifters)

1. Rothschild (Bauer) - Pindar
2. Bruce
3. Cavendish (Kennedy)
4. de Medici
5. Hanover
6. Hapsburg
7. Krupps
8. Plantagenet
9. Rockefeller
10. Romanov
11. Sinclair / St. Clair
12. Warburg (del Banco)
13. Windsor (Saxe - Coburg - Gothe)

Committee of 300 (Families)

Sexuality & Mind-Pattern

Since there is only one Universal Mind and It is All There Is in existence, it follows that all acts on every level represent patterns from that Mind. Since the Mind is singular, despite its many apparent fragmentations, all beings are androgynous. Separation of the so-called sexes occurs only during the drop to the physical level. A true personification of left-brain (female) and right-brain (male) thinking is represented by Adam and Eve; yin and yang; and positive and negative magnetism.

In physical reality, heterosexuality is an illusion. When there are forms of homosexuality there is a change in the mind-pattern of the Mind of God. How could two female energies create anything? The same goes for male energies. Given the fact of polarization of male and female energies, the two same sex energies should repel each other rather than attract. One of the entities is actually polarized incorrectly, i.e., a female energy has incarnated in a male body, or vice versa.

This occurs for several reasons. A last minute switch before entry of a soul with predominantly female energy suddenly decides to incarnate in a male body, but does not adjust the ratios of the male and female energies can create a homosexual mind-pattern. An influence of simultaneous lives of one sex while the entity in this one is the opposite, can create a homosexual mind-pattern. Another reason is the need for the soul-personality to overcome an influence so it needs to incarnate in a particular sex even though its mind-pattern is of the opposite sex.

Other reasons include genetic manipulation, mind control, and walk-in personalities. Most of these involve DNA types that can be scientifically proven. For any reason listed above, correction is necessary, and all involve mind-patterns of self-worth. Bisexuality is actually a greater realization of the mind-pattern since there really is no male or female gender in God-Mind.

Any sexual act represents a replay or reenactment of creation in the Mind of God and is merely an attempt to balance mind-pattern. The attraction of male and female is the mind-pattern for reunification. The act of an erect penis penetrating a vagina is symbolic of a vortex of energy opening a pathway to physical reality. On a physical level, orgasm in the male represents the release of a thought from the Mind of God to create, while orgasm in a female represents physical reality receiving the energies of God and using these energies to create life. The act of a kiss is symbolic of the beginning of life when two cells attach to one another to exchange DNA.

A single male ejaculation contains enough seed to populate worlds. Over a lifetime, one man produces infinite seed, symbolic of the potential for multiple creations without boundaries. A female has a limited number of eggs to use in her lifetime, symbolic of the finiteness of physical reality. A female's ability to reproduce is only from puberty to menopause, while the male can reproduce until his physical death.

When a man is brutal with a woman, such as a rape or even a beating, it represents an attempt to overpower the ego. All sexual dysfunctions stem from this. Impotence stems from a fear of confronting the ego. All sexual disease represent lack of self-worth and denial of being. Menstrual disorders represent self-dislike of femininity. A heavy flow of blood represents the loss of joy of being a woman.

Think of the gestation period of a human being—nine months. In those nine months, the entire range of human evolution is produced from one single cell, to sea life, to reptilian life, to mammalian life. Careful monitoring of these stages allows one to observe every phase of genetic manipulation that has occurred within mankind. Even the act of nursing symbolically represents the child receiving programming information from his/her mother.

When a child is born with Mongoloidism, there is significant alien genetic material within the DNA of that child. In fact, any physical abnormality in a newborn shows evidence of his/her frequency. Sudden Infant Death Syndrome occurs when the personality changes its mind entering that body, so it leaves abruptly. The soul-personality does not enter the new body until the first breath.

The womb filled with saline water is symbolic of the ocean origin of life. The soft spot on the top of a baby's head, called the fontanel, is symbolic of the blowhole of a whale or dolphin. All this evidence is right in front of everyone, yet not understood. Why are some babies born with webbed hands and feet? Why are tears salt water? Why do you get goose bumps? All of this is proof of your amphibian ancestry.

Chromosomal Influences:

XX = Female, Symbolic of Multiplication and Cancellation For a female, there is a choice to either multiply or cancel the left-brain. XY = Male, Symbolic of Multiplication of the Mind of God. For a male, there is also choice. His chromosomal instructions are to multiply or cancel the right-brain.

News Clips from *Expansions Exposé*

December 2000
Wall Street Warning

Last Friday's sudden drop in the Stock Market foretells the major plummet that I expect within the next few months. Microsoft warned of a global economic slowdown which sent he Standard & Poor's 500 Index to its lowest point in more than a year. Intel Corporation, Eastman-Kodak, GM, and Chase Manhattan Corporation, all Illuminati-Nazi corporations, have warned of the drop. They are telling what will happen. Is anyone listening? I would not keep any funds in the Stock Market until further notice. They are planning a global financial crisis at your expense and it will happen suddenly as a result of a global threat. Take heed. You have been warned.

December 2000
It Has Begun!

Readers will remember my warnings a few weeks ago about power shortages due to the release of reserves, and my predictions of severe weather from the Great Lakes to the Northeast. Well, it has begun. Seattle area newspapers are warning customers about severe power outages and low fuel supplies that are depleted. Cold waves in the Northwest have strained reserves that are normally bolstered by supplies from California. However, California is in trouble due to the severe heat of the past summer, as well as the cold snap that is using up their reserves.

In addition, extreme cold and heavy snows have engulfed the Midwest and is moving east. Chicago airports have been virtually shut down. Buffalo New York experienced its third worst snowstorm in November. The season has just begun and I expect it to be a humdinger! Better finish knitting those comforters and saving candles!

December 2000
Queen of Hearts

Many readers and those who have come to my lectures have heard me say that within six to twelve months people will start seeing and channeling the late Princess Diana, creating an icon of the New World Religion. I was wrong. It is happening now! There is a new book titled "The Celestial Voice of Diana" by Findhorn Press, which was channeled by a Norwegian woman named Rita Eide.

To give you a synopsis of this extensive document, "Diana" claims:

—She was the mother of the Virgin Mary in a past life, thereby making her Jesus' grandmother.

—The true name of Jesus, as I have previously stated, is "Emmanuel" She is now in charge of "love" energy on Earth, making her the Queen of Hearts

—The royal family are "blue-bloods" who are survivors from an ancient past (reptilians??)

—Describes Lemuria as the first place colonized on the Earth (you've heard that from me before)

—Tells how alien beings manipulated human DNA (Duh!)

—The Star Tetrahedron is a universal form of alight body (is she channeling Drunvelo?)

—Refused to discuss her family relationships

All very interesting. Diana and Christ. The new male/female icons of the N.W.O. Global Religion!

On a side note, recently on the front cover of a British newspaper was a picture of Prince William giving the "Devil's Greeting" with his hand! The stage is set. Curtain up.

January 2001
Chinese Take-Out

This past week, mainland China allowed ferries from Taiwan to dock and bring passengers. It is a further sign of unification of Chinese territories, a precursor to aggressive behavior that will manifest shortly.

January 2001
So Tsunami

As above, so below. As on the East Coast, so on the West Coast. Readers are referred to my previous article on a possible tsunami generated by La Palma volcano for the East Coast of the US. Now scientists are warning residents from Santa Barbara to Santa Monica that an ocean quake and resultant undersea mud slide could generate a tsunami for the Southern California coastline. Most residents of the area don't even realize that the entire western portion of the state is supported by undersea columns of rock that could collapse at any time, and eventually will. Be prepared.

January 2001
Western China/Israel

On New Year's Day, Newsday ran an article about the Moslems in Urumzi, China being of non-oriental heritage and wanting to separate from China. The article said that the local people would fight the Chinese army and the Han ethnic Chinese who are being pushed into this area. The stage is now set and publicized for the Chinese attack on the Moslems. On New Year's Eve, the son of Israeli Militant Meir Kahane and his wife were machined gunned to death by Palestinian extremists. Jews in Jerusalem and West Bank settlements vowed to kill all Palestinians in revenge. Now the West and East of Asia have been ignited.

February 2001
Terran Tidbits

The Arctic: The tundra permafrost is melting at an alarming rate, releasing greenhouse gases that have been trapped for thousands of years. An ice sheet the size of Massachusetts broke off the glacial covering. The increase of carbon gases will cause an increase in temperatures that will affect weather patterns.

Asia: Japan is preparing for an eruption of Mt. Fuji as magma bubbling to the surface caused nearly 500 tremors within the last 2 months. In Indonesia, the Merapi Volcano threatens a major explosion.

Britain: Peacocks are running amok looking for mates. An overpopulation of these birds has caused them to chase children and destroy gardens as they desperately seek partners.

Los Angeles : Yours truly experienced a wide range of disasters this past week in "sunny" California. The sky dumped several inches of rain on the city causing mudslides and floods. The mountains nearby received several feet of snow. A water spout was seen and filmed off the coast, and a 5.1 earthquake topped off the week's unstable conditions. I remained secure in the Hollywood Hills.

Mt. Baker, Washington State: A plume of volcano smoke was released over the weekend, foretelling a possible eruption in the near future.

February 2001
Anti-Arctic

Satellite surveillance has shown that 7.5 cubic miles of ice have melted from the ice sheets over Antarctica. Scientists say that at the present rate of shrinkage, it would take centuries for the oceans to rise significantly enough to worry. If the entirety melted from the entire continent of Antarctica, the oceans would rise 240 feet, submerging all present coastlines and most low lying islands. It would be wise for scientists to check the rising temperatures of Jupiter, which will be a second sun by 2010. That should melt the ice sheets rather quickly!

March 2001
Buddha Bashing

In Afghanistan, the recent declaration by the Taliban to destroy ancient statues is part of the overall plan to incite the non-Moslem world against the Moslem fundamentalists. This will contribute fuel to the planned, upcoming war in the Middle East.

Excerpts
Belief Systems Shattered

By Janet Swerdlow

All Experiences Are Neutral...
Even Alien Invasions & N.W.O. Agendas!

Whatever experience comes into your life is a result of your own mind-pattern. Nothing can come to you unless you invite it, no matter how horrendous it may seem. On some level, there is a part of you that needs the experience for balance and growth. The more horrendous it is, the more you learn, stretch, and grow. You are forced to dip into the deepest resources that you can possibly access. These experiences are great teachers filled with an infinite amount of knowledge.

Remember, all experience is neutral. It is your reactions that label the experience "good" or "bad." When you have a positive reaction to an experience, you label the experience "good." When you have a negative reaction, you label the experience "bad." But, the experience itself remains neutral.

For instance, if a small child gets lost in the forest, he will find the forest intimidating and overwhelming. The child will describe the forest as dark, dreary, lonely, and scary. Because he associates the feeling of being lost with the forest, he labels the forest "bad."

However, when he becomes an adult he enjoys walking alone in the stillness of the forest. He now associates the forest with feelings of peace and calm. Now, he labels the forest "good."

Through both experiences, the forest remains neutral, yet both positive and negative experiences define a forest. And, the forest is a part of God-Mind that exists as an experience in physical reality.

All experiences filter through an infinite number of simultaneous lifetimes. When you explore the multidimensional levels, you do find connections. Once you begin an experience, you explore it in every conceivable way, with every conceivable beginning and ending, including everything in between. This means that before it concludes within your soul-personality, you will understand it on all levels until you realize that the experience itself is neutral. You only used the experience to learn, grow, and explore yourself, and ultimately, God-Mind.

This is the key - *you* use the experience, while not allowing the experience to use you.

You use the experience to find out who and what you are, what you can and cannot do, where you are in balance and out of balance. Glean everything that you possibly can from the one experience until your reaction is neutral. When you realize that the experience is neutral you reach the end of the ride, or the beginning of it, however you choose to view it.

Most people do not do this, and that is why they continue to repeat the same experiences over and over again. As long as something is out of balance in your mind-pattern, you will continually set up tests for yourself to bring that part of Self back into balance. Because God-Mind is neutral, you must eventually also return to the neutral position. You are only a microcosm of the macrocosm.

The same is true of everything, including alien invasions and N.W.O. agendas. These are experiences that you are helping to generate from some level of your mind-pattern. If it were not in your mind-pattern, you would not be here. You came here at this particular moment in time and space to participate in this experience. *How* you experience it and what you learn from it is entirely up to you. You do not have to go to a science fiction movie when you realize that you are creating your own movie right here and now! You have elected to participate in your own story, whatever that may be, and so have your loved ones and friends.

You do have a choice regarding how you choose to move through this experience. Will you use it for its ultimate knowledge and growth, or will you allow it to use you? Physical reality is designed to bring you down, and it will certainly do that if you let it. Your challenge is to move through it, through the collective unconscious, or, group-mind, and into individualized consciousness, where you are in total control of your own mind-pattern.

Individualized consciousness means that you are now above the energy of the group-mind. You moved through it, explored it, and understand it. Now, you can turn around and use the group-mind without it using, or controlling, you.

While possible, this move to individualized consciousness will most likely not happen on a mass scale. That is why it is so easy to manipulate people through group-mind control. People are controlled every day by the type of cars they drive, clothes they wear, food they eat, form of worship, etc. "They" herd people around in every live facet, and "they" know it. Your life is controlled, and you are so used to it that you do not even take the time to stop and recognize it. This is exactly what "they" intend.

If you *do* begin to recognize this, there is always another direction to throw you off guard, such as the proliferation of New Age disinformation, discrediting of valid information, and outright targeting of those who get too close to the truth.

Always remember, that because someone can do something, or see something, does not make them spiritual, or a positive force! It simply means that they have access to a recipe that you do not! When you have a cake recipe, and you follow that recipe, you will get a cake. It does not matter if you are "good" or "bad," you will still get a cake.

When you see that cake, you forget about the baker. You only remember that you see a cake. Because you do not know how to make one, you consider the event "miraculous." And, because only "good" people are equated with miracles, you forget to go beyond the cake. You are now an open candidate to be controlled by this person, or whatever it is that emanates this person.

Even when that person appears to be doing "good" things for the "right" reasons, you must continually be a skeptical force, peering beyond the obvious. Examine everyone and everything until you *know by knowing* who and what propels that person.

"They" want you to go outside for your answers, because this is the only way that you can be controlled. Once you discover your own power, you can go beyond the cake, beyond the baker, and into the unseen levels. Then you will have your own knowledge and you will be independent, without the need, desire, or mind-pattern, for anyone else to control you.

Is Your Reaction Fear?

Do you react with fear when you think about the possibilities of the "future?" That is considered a positive reaction by those who wish to control you, for fear is what "they" feed from. Remember, every thought you think creates and emanates energy. Fear emanates a specific kind of energy. When enough people generate fear energy, "they" are energized by it and know how to use it for their own purpose (positive) and against the populace (negative). They harness the energy, magnify and amplify it, then direct it to their target with exponential force.

Everyone knows that when they are around an angry animal, that animal feels your fear. The more fearful you are, the more empowered it becomes. Essentially, it feeds off your fear, growing more vicious. As it grows more vicious, you grow more fearful, and the cycle continues to feed itself. This is the type of cycle that is now being set up with regard to the "future."

Everything that you are now hearing about already existed before you were consciously aware of the information. Now that you are hearing about it, you have the opportunity to do something. You cannot fix something if you do not realize that it needs fixing. Allow yourself to experience your emotions, whatever they may be. Pass them up to your Oversoul as you feel them, moving them out of your auric field.

When you finish emoting, stand in your center as an objective observer of the situation. Your ability to remain objective allows you to think clearly about the choices that you have to make.

First, it is important for you to find the weak areas of your own mind-pattern; the places that allow others to control you. Once you find those areas, you can make them stronger and close the gaps.

Take a look around yourself, and find out what controls you. Do you control your eating habits, or do they control you? Do you control your anger, or does it control you? Do you control your fear, or does it control you?

You do not want to get rid of fear, because a certain amount of fear is healthy; it keeps you cautious and alert. But you do not want to move beyond fear into panic or paranoia. Panic and paranoia are fear amplified and magnified. This is the reaction that creates the energy that others can use.

Think about your smallest fears, because those are the easiest for you to control. Perhaps you have a fear of being late, getting lost, not having "enough", not finding the right job or relationship, the list can go on and on when you spend some time thinking about it.

Replace that mind-pattern with *I am always on time, I always know my way, I always have enough, I find the right job and/or relationship, etc.* By changing the lessor fears in your life, you will understand how to find and face the larger fears.

Think of your worst fears that send you into a panic. Then, in your mind, work through that situation. Breathe yourself into your center. Anchor Self in Oversoul and God-Mind. Review the situation, experience and learn from it, and then release it back up to your Oversoul. Watch the fear energy flow and flow and flow. Allow yourself to trace that mind-pattern back to its origin. Forgive everyone, including yourself, that needs to be forgiven. Relive the original experience as many times as needed until you feel neutral and objective about it. Understand the positive and negative aspects to put your mind-pattern in balance. Next, replace the old mind-pattern that you just released with a new mind-pattern, such as, *I release the need to be a victim, I am always safe and secure, my family is always safe and secure, etc.*

When you are willing to face your fears, they disappear. You no longer have a need for a physical experience to bring you knowledge and growth. You gleaned the information through your mental work. When you allow fear to use you, know that others can use your fear to control, manipulate, and harm you.

How come a particular person, home, business, or building is selected for a crime when there are plenty of others to choose from? Is it random? Or do its occupants hold a specific mind-pattern that attracts the crime to it? On some level, is the mind-pattern of the occupants seeking out someone or something who will bring them the experience they need?

These thoughts are not comfortable thoughts. No one wants to think that he/she invites negative experiences into his/her lives. But it is often these negative experiences that are your greatest teachers. They force you to face areas of yourself that you previously overlooked. They force change, whether you are consciously ready for change or not.

Learn to be proactive instead of reactive. Search in your own mind-pattern. Look for your own weaknesses. Bring them out, look at them, find their origin, correct and balance them. Be your own teacher instead of waiting for someone else to teach you.

There are many examples throughout history of people who have gone through horrendous group experiences seemingly unscathed and relatively untouched by them. Yes, these group experiences do affect the masses because they are designed by the mind-pattern of the collective unconscious of the masses. It is those few who have reached places of individualized consciousness who move through the group experiences relatively easier.

You can do the same. Be mindful of the mind-patterns that you generate. Be honest with yourself. Recognize that you contain both positive and negative. Do not avoid the negative because you think that it is "bad." Negative is simply negative. Know that with the correct mind-pattern, you will pull the correct outer experiences to yourself.

Subverting Sexuality

Sexual energy is the most powerful creative energy available in physical reality. When properly used by the correct combination of people, the possibilities for creation are endless. The powers that be know this, and they are out to systematically subvert sexual energy to keep it in an animalistic arena.

Blatant sexuality is all around, from fashion to media to everyday speech. This sexuality is a deep, bright red that essentially pulls on your sexual chakras and opens them up. Using color, tone, and archetype (or symbol), these chakras are systematically opened, fed, and energized, expanding them out of proportion until they have control over you. Then, you are controlled and manipulated through these chakras.

If someone wants to sell something, they simply link it into sex. This is a well-known fact among sellers and purchasers alike. Your desires are constantly manipulated through sex. You are sold all kinds of goods and services based upon your supposed sexual need for them. Even ideas are sold to you through sex.

Girls as young as 6 and 7 years old are beginning their menstrual cycles. Some say that it is due to the extensive use of growth hormones in the meat products.

Much of popular music is designed to open up the root chakras. The vibratory rate automatically opens up your chakra system, and the body responds to the beat, feeding the stage for undirected sexual interest and activity, as well as frustration and anger.

You are purposefully opened to allow in all of the highly charged, animalistic sexual innuendoes and activities surrounding you. This makes you open and subject to control by anything on that frequency.

This leads to incorrect "coupling". People are allowing their sexuality to use them instead of them using their sexuality. Sexual activity is taking place too early in relationships and for the wrong reasons. This premature sexual coupling leads to unwanted and unplanned pregnancies, especially among the young. It also increases the risks for sexual disease and sexual dysfunction later in life.

Correct coupling sets the stage for the best combination of DNA and genetics for future generations. If people utilize this knowledge, they will consciously create a race of aware human beings. When the frequencies of the parents are a proper match, the couple will automatically have a more viable, stable relationship. This in turn means less interpersonal difficulties, creating a more stable home. A child born of that union has a better chance for physical, mental, emotional, and spiritual health. A child born of that union will move vertically toward its Source, instead of the continual horizontal pull, and sometimes downward spiral, that now takes place.

Our present system simply produces children as potential workers, as the powers that be see all people. They do not want people that are too aware, too healthy, too stable, or too connected to God-Mind. This kind of person will see their agenda and refuse to be a part of it. A person here or there is not such a problem, but an entire race is.

The reality is that each sexual position has a specific function. Specific positions create specific results. Specific colors, tones, and archetypes also create specific results. Sexual energy can be purposefully directed to create whatever you desire in physical reality. Sexual energy can be used to create on the hyperspace level when the couple is linked into God-Mind using specific color codes, archetypes, and sounds

The Reptilians know all this, except they use sex to create on the astral level, and bring that into physical reality. They do not want the common populace to have or know this information. That is why major religions have so many rules about sexuality, which seems to almost always include instilling guilt.

For example, the bible tells you basically to use sex only for procreation, and major religions primarily advocate only one position. The powers that be did not want any purposeful sex other than the continuation of the worker line. They did not/do not want people to discover the true nature of sex. They do not want you exploring the higher realms of sexuality because you may discover the true purpose of sex in physical reality.

When the "sexual revolution" came about, then they simply directed sexuality into something that would never serve a purpose except on the most base levels. Whatever society wants, they are given in such a way that their own wants and desires are fulfilled. Once fulfilled, then these desires are turned against the people to control and manipulate them. Recognize that sexuality as it is presented in the outer world is just another way to take your innermost desires, subvert them, and then use them against you.

In addition, all of this haphazard sexuality is creating a sexual energy force that is being harnessed by the Reptilians to use toward their own purposes. The more sexual energy that is generated, the more powerful they become. Without knowing how to recalibrate your sexual chakra bands, you are open to anything on that frequency.

Keep an eye on your own sexual chakra bands to ensure that they stay a pale red, rather than a deep, bright red. Also keep the second chakra band pale orange, as in its agitated state it is a deep, bright orange. This will enhance the physical health of the areas, as well as your mental well-being. It will also help you focus on the frequency of your correct life partner as you wade through the dense, sexual atmosphere that is purposefully created to fool you into mistaking a myriad of feelings for love.

Learn to use your mind to control your sexuality, rather than letting it control you. Understand that this intense, creative force has a purpose beyond the survival instinct. Walk through the pitfalls that are purposefully designed to ensnare and trap you in this reality. To move on to the higher levels, you must first release your need to explore only the lower levels. Know that, as with all things, this force is infinitely deep, and is waiting for you to explore it in multidimensional ways that you cannot as yet even imagine.

Vegetarianism—Is It Really The Way?

All the food that is available for human consumption is a creation, or reflection, of the mind-pattern of the human collective unconscious mind.

Some people do not want to eat flesh foods because they do not like the idea of killing animals. If you object to killing animals, then you should also object to killing plants, because it is a proven fact that they also have consciousness, and that they feel fear when threatened, and pain when harmed. What is the difference, then, between killing an animal and killing a plant for consumption?

The truth is that the soul of any food that is eaten knows that it is here for this purpose. The soul-personalities that inhabit these forms of life are also in a state of evolution. They learn about who and what they are from their experiences and interaction with humans. Allow them to be what they are, rather than force your judgement of what you **think** they are and should be. Instead, come from a place of **knowing.** Before plants and animals are killed for food, they are prepared on the inner levels. Their souls are already gone.

Often, people think that other life forms hold the same consciousness as humans. In general, the consciousness of animals are not as fully present in the body as the human consciousness. The state that they operate in is more similar to the human dream state. This is true of plant life as well.

Plants and animals are cared for and cultivated. It may not be what you would want for yourself, as a human, but there is a reason for all that other life forms go through. When you are in touch with your Oversoul and God-Mind, all of this is explained to you in the state of **knowing by knowing**.

Sometimes people choose to be vegetarians because they view it as "more spiritual." More spiritual than what? And by whose definition? Sometimes people use their vegetarianism as an excuse to "look down" on others who choose not to follow the same life choice. On some level, they believe this condescension elevates their own spirituality.

People who are vegetarians often try to force something on the body that it is not ready for. Yes, you have control, but that is not what this reality is about. Your physical body is your vehicle and partner of your soul-personality. It has a consciousness. When you take control over your body to the extreme, you ignore that consciousness and its right to exist in optimum health and well-being. Even the auric fields of vegetarians are often weaker than flesh-eaters.

Sometimes vegetarians are drooling on the inside over the desire for a piece of meat, but force the body to ignore the cravings. Your body knows more about its care than you do. Learn to listen to its needs and feed it accordingly. You will know when it is time to eat and not eat. Vegetarians often control the body to the extreme without balance.

The human body requires flesh food to properly build itself and replicate its DNA. Think about the warriors and people of physical strength. Are they vegetarians or meat-eaters? Do you think the powers that be want your body strong or weak? Do you think they want you to be a meat-eater or a vegetarian? Which would serve their purpose the best?

Are your eating decisions emotion or logic based? How does your body feel with/without flesh foods? Does it crave something but you deny the body what it needs?

When you are in touch with your body, you know what it needs at all times for optimum health. You know when it needs flesh food and when it does not. You know if it needs red meat, fowl, or fish. You know if it needs some other form of protein, such as beans, legumes, or dairy.

You know if it needs fruits or vegetables, and grains, as well as which ones. You know when it needs sugars and starches. Your body consciousness will instruct you on how to care and keep the body healthy if you let it.

Sometimes becoming a vegetarian for a while is a good choice. It helps clean out the internal organs. But do talk to your body and find out when and if it wants to consume flesh foods again. Do not deny your body the right to exist in optimal health. Do not force your will upon it just because you can.

If you are a vegetarian, or considering becoming one, think about your particular choice. Talk to your body, and see what it needs. You may be surprised at the answers.

Are You A "Sleeper?"

A "sleeper" is usually thought of as a mind-controlled individual who is programmed to perform a specific task at a specific time after activation using a specific code of some type. In general, the word "sleeper" has a negative connotation, and that is what the powers that be want you to think. You would not want to be a sleeper would you?

Or *would* you?? Maybe not all sleepers are programmed for destruction. Maybe this planet is filled with individuals who are positive sleepers, waiting to be activated so that they can rise up, join thought energy, and change the course of history.

Most sleepers never feel like they belong. That is because they do not. They do not belong to the herd mentality, and never will no matter how hard they try. And some have tried extremely hard with devastating personal consequences.

Have you cloistered yourself because others do not understand you? Have you allowed your inner greatness and power to die down within yourself because you know if you let it out you would so outshine everyone around you that you would never be accepted?

Do you realize that the reason that the wise man goes to live in the mountains is not because the wise man cannot stand the people, but because the people cannot stand the wise man? When the people see a true wise man, it makes them look at themselves and their own shortcomings and failures. Because they cannot stand to look at themselves, the wise man makes them uncomfortable. They do not welcome him with open arms, waiting to learn from him. They make him an outcast so that they do not have to deal with themselves, for he is a reflection of their potential.

The people would rather have false leaders, for it is far easier. Then they can be led down a path that is more familiar, thus more comfortable. Why move out of familiarity? Why become uncomfortable? And, while they may protest, a dictatorship is more efficient and an easier place to be. Someone to tell you what to do and when to do it.

How many of you have ever consulted a "psychic" because you want to know if you should: marry someone, divorce someone, date someone, stop seeing someone, see a certain doctor, not see a certain doctor, move to a new location, stay in your current location, buy a house, rent an apartment, change jobs, not change jobs, etc, etc.

And, if you consulted a psychic, did you stop with one? Or did you ask several the same question? And, are you still looking for the perfect psychic? Do you think that the ones that charge the most money are the best? Can you buy your answers from someone?? After all, isn't that easier than finding your own answer?

At some point, everyone looks for someone to tell them what to do! Why? Because it is the easiest way out of any situation! But because it is the easiest does not make it the best solution!

People *do* need to be led. But the reason is because that is how we help each other. There is always someone on the next rung of the ladder above you who can reach back and give you a hand. And, there is someone on the rung of the ladder behind you to whom you can reach back and give a hand. But to find that helping hand, you must look above you, and move vertically, not horizontally. Horizontal movements do not pull you up on your quest. They only distract you from finding the help you really seek. People need to be led into their upliftment, not into their enslavement.

If others feel insecure around you, that is their problem, not yours. Have compassion for them, offer your hand, but if they refuse to take it, do not force the issue. Hold your head up and keep moving forward. There is an old saying, "Don't cast your pearls before swine."

The more you allow yourself to be exactly who you designed yourself to be, the more opportunities exist for others to find out who they are. Let them be uncomfortable. Let them feel insecure. Whoever said that growth is comfortable? It is not your place to learn their lessons for them. You can guide, but you cannot take on their lessons, because if you do, you are the only one who learns. Let their feelings of discomfort and insecurity be their teachers. Give them motivation for looking at themselves.

What is your function here? Why did you choose to come in these turbulent times?

Are you a leader but you have never taken the time to recognize it? Being a leader is the loneliest job available. You have the most responsibility, everyone scrutinizes your every move. The true leader has the least freedom. The true leader has great moral and ethical responsibility.

Be a leader wherever you are, whatever your position in life. Humanity needs leaders who are sleepers to awaken now. How else will the masses have access to *true* leadership unless the leaders live and work among them, and know what the people need and want? Make yourself available where you are right now. Do not wish you were "somewhere else, in a more spiritual career." Redefine your definition of "leader" and "teacher." These are not formal positions!

Do you want to add to the upliftment of the collective unconscious mind? Do you want to be a way-show-er for others to follow? Or do you want to hide in the comfort of the herd mentality? And that includes "New Age" herd mentality! Is it just "peace, love, and light?" Is it "vegetarianism?" Is it "channeling?" Or "crystals?" Or whatever happens to be "in" at the moment? Whatever you do, *know* what you are doing and why!

You can do some very bad things even with the best of intentions when you do not know what you are doing! Often people think that something is better than nothing, but that is totally incorrect. Don't go for the short-term effect, go for the long-term.

Are you adding to the degradation of humanity or to its upliftment? What kind of lifestyle do you have? Is it a positive one with direct purpose? Is it full of fluff-n-stuff that looks great on the outside, but leaves you empty on the inside? Are you settling for ideals that others bestow upon you, or goals that others give you?

When enough people wake up from their sleep to realize that they are here to feel their own strength and power in conjunction with the strength and power of their Oversouls and God-Mind, watch out, because there is a new world coming!

Illuminati As Teachers

If everyone and everything is a reflection of your own mind-pattern, then it follows that the Illuminati are also only reflections of your own mind-pattern. As such, are they to be feared and reviled as some would have you believe? Or are they to be studied and learned from so that you will understand your own mind-pattern?

Why do you choose to co-exist with them at this time? What are they teaching you about yourself? The majority of people are oblivious to the fact that they even exist. Simply the "discovery" of their existence is an accomplishment, considering how cleverly they disguise themselves. Congratulate yourself on reaching that level of knowledge and potential self-understanding. After all, it takes a skilled teacher to teach an intelligent student.

If they are so evil, why do they appear to have the best that physical reality has to offer, and not you? They, too, are surrounded by reflections of their own mind-patterns. Their mind-patterns are bringing them the best entertainment, the best homes, access to the best medical care, the best education, the best political offices, the best financial resources, the best emergency resources, the best human resources, the best security, the best transportation, etc.

They have the purest crystals and gems. They can travel to any part of the world any time they wish, often at taxpayer expense.

They hire bodyguards, personal shoppers, cooks, nannies, housekeepers, drivers, gardeners, body workers, plastic surgeons, hairstylists, make-up artists, personal trainers, and fashion designers.

They do not send their children off to public schools, or to war, except as behind-the-lines strategists.

They have access to secret information on all levels about everything. They believe that they have the right to direct the course of humanity, and they do.

What do they have that you do not? If "peace, love, and light" are all you need for good things to happen, then why does it outwardly appear that the other side is winning all the rewards?

What is the difference between the Illuminati and you?

They do not have a victim mentality. Their mind-patterns tell them that they are invincible. They believe that no one can stop them.

They do not have an inferiority complex. They do not feel "less than" anyone.

They do not have low self-worth issues. No one can make them feel bad about themselves.

They do not have guilt issues. They believe they are justified in everything that they do.

They do not have issues of lack. They know they have the time and resources for whatever they need.

They do not live in denial. They know who and what they are, and are proud of it.

They do not place limitations on themselves. They believe that they are limitless, and prove this every day. They can reach anyone, anywhere on the globe, and beyond, at any time.

They do have high levels of self-worth. Not only do family and friends reinforce this, but so does the media, and the average person on the street. People everywhere honor them wherever they go, wanting to be included in their lives in some way, no matter how small.

They do believe that they are superior. There is no doubt in their minds about how great they are. They even segregate themselves from the rest of society. They interact with others outside their circles only enough to garner the support of the masses.

They do believe that they deserve the best. They have the best that physical reality has to offer, as previously stated.

They do have a winner's mentality. There is no question in their minds that they will win at whatever they set out to do, even if it takes years. They carefully lay out their plans, and strategically carry it out on a global scale.

They do know their purpose. They do not have to search for their purpose. There is no doubt in their mind what they are here to do.

They do know that they have secret knowledge. They can access any information that they need about anything at any time, as well as make decisions about what to reveal to the masses.

They do know that they have the power to influence society. They do not sit around thinking about how to do it "some day." They do it now!

They do have a global consciousness. They view the entire world as their playground. They are not myopic in any way.

These mind-patterns, and more, are a natural part of who and what they are. All of these mind-patterns are reinforced every minute that they breathe. Think about this. Learn from them. Know their strengths, because this is what they will use against you. Know your weaknesses, because this is what they will use against you. They will teach you, if you let them. Learn now from a proactive stance rather than later from a reactive stance.

When you change your mind-pattern, the reflection must change. When this happens, you will no longer perceive the Illuminati as a threat. They will instead be remembered as beings who took the time to teach you about who and what you really are. In the meantime, study them closely. They are some of your greatest teachers.

Victim Mentality

This planet primarily attracts two types of beings—those with a victim mentality and those with an oppressor mentality. In order to be a victim, you must have oppressors. In order to be an oppressor, you must have victims. Together, this creates balance in God-Mind.

This planet is designed as a place where beings with a victim mentality can learn to overcome it. Therefore, any "higher level" being will not become involved because it is necessary for those here to have the opportunity to work through their victim mentalities. To become involved would mean interfering or taking away the lessons of those with victim mentalities. Higher level beings will be objective observers who will guide and instruct you through your victim mentality once you reach them, but that is all. They are not here to "save" you or this planet.

Any being who says that they are here to "save" you is interfering in your soul growth. Only you can "save" yourself from a victim mentality. Only you and the lessons you self-design will teach you about victim mentality. Only you can move through these lessons that will allow you to make a final release of your victim mentality. No one is waiting to help you—do not be fooled by any being making such promises.

When you learn to move through your victim mentality, your mind-pattern will no longer attract oppressors. The more stubborn you are in your determination to hang onto your victim mentality ways, the more intense the lessons that you attract to get you to release those ways. This means, metaphorically speaking, a bigger, meaner, stronger, stick until you finally "get it."

You have to get hurt, belittled, and finally, angry enough to stand up for yourself and declare that you will no longer be a victim to anyone, anywhere, any more! Perhaps when you finally have had enough, you release your victim mentality by saying, "I just don't give a damn anymore what anybody thinks! I am speaking my mind regardless! I am taking care of myself, regardless!"

Sometimes, people are beaten up so much that instead of releasing the victim mentality, they decide to become the oppressor when the opportunity presents itself. This is why cycles repeat themselves. People who were oppressed find other victims, because this gives them a sense of control. In doing so, they relive their earlier experiences when they felt like they had no control. They become the perpetrator, just so they can be the "winner" for a change. Of course, this is another imbalance, or extreme flip from victim to oppressor.

The ideal is to find a happy medium, or balance, between victim and oppressor. Victim and oppressor are opposite sides of the same coin in the Mind of God. In this case, two individual soul-personalities are needed to maintain an equilibrium in God-Mind. One carries the weight of a victim, one carries the weight of an oppressor. What you need to do is find the balance within yourself, so that equilibrium within the Mind of God is maintained within one soul-personality instead of two.

Yes, you must learn to speak your mind and not allow anyone to walk on you. Yes, you must sometimes be harsh and cruel with words and sometimes even actions. But when this must happen, it must be done in an objective manner—what is best for everyone involved to get the point across while causing the least amount of pain. Boundaries must be set.

What are your boundaries? Who crosses them and how? Who is a belligerent person in your life that you try to avoid because of their bullish, pushy ways? Why do you avoid this person? Why not practice letting go of your victim mentality and speak your mind to him/her? So what if your heart races and palpitates, and your palms grow sweaty? So what if your knees shake so hard that you think you will fall down, and your voice is shaky, squeaky, or barely audible? Somewhere along the way, you must stop your victim mentality before it stops you. Learn to be proactive instead of reactive.

When you allow others to push you around, you become angry, sullen, and introverted. Then, you lash out at the undeserving with misdirected frustration and anger. Sometimes your body becomes ill because of all that you suppress, or you insulate your body, or perhaps stop eating. One way or the other, you suffer.

But, there is a part of you that feels that you deserve to suffer. There is a part of you that enjoys this pain and self-punishment. It feels good to some part of yourself, or you would not do it. Some people create others to give them pain, sometimes physical, sometimes emotional, sometimes both. Some people do it for themselves—a self-contained, fully functional, victim mentality unit. Some people are extremely successful at this.

Why do you feel so bad about yourself that you feel like you are meant to suffer, to be alone, to feel guilty, to have ill health, to be over- or underweight? Did it start in this lifetime, or did it start before? Follow those feelings, and allow yourself to release it. This physical reality is your chance to overcome it. The more you ignore this situation, the harder and more intense lesson you will attract to beat it out of yourself. You came here to learn now do it. Quit whining, moaning, and complaining because there is a part of you that enjoys that too.

Aches and pains can create a lot of entertainment. You can run from doctor to doctor, trying to find a cure for something that will never be cured as long as you maintain your current mind-pattern.

"Bad luck" can attract a lot of attention and sympathy from others. Dire circumstances will force someone to pay attention to you. Never getting a raise or a promotion is an excuse not to climb higher in your career or company. You can moan all you want about being alone, with a partner who does not understand you, or without one at all. But this self-imposed isolation also gives you time to selfishly take care of yourself without any interference. The same for saying you want children but are unable to have them. A part of you does not want a spouse, or a caring spouse, or children, because if ALL of you wanted this and it was truly in your mind-pattern, you would have it!

Victim, victim, victim! Let us count the ways...Refuse to be a victim. Find a new source of entertainment. Release yourself from this mind-pattern so that you can move into new vistas of growth—ones so vast that you cannot even imagine or comprehend them. You must let go of the old to make room for the new. No one can do it for you. No one can "save" you from yourself. No one is waiting to help this planet. Only you can make a difference. Only you can save this planet. Do it!

Are You A Mind-Control Candidate?

Does mind-control sound like a foreboding subject that people in dark, mysterious places practice upon unsuspecting victims? Do you read about other people's claims with interest, while thinking that it really has nothing to do with you? Remember, if you are reading about it, it is in your world. If it is in your world, it is a reflection of some part of yourself or it could not exist. So, are you a mind-control candidate for sinister forces?

To fit the profile they are looking for, you must be controllable. Are you? What does your mind-pattern look like? Are you in control of your life, or is your life in control of you?

If anything, anywhere controls you, you have an established mind-pattern that any force can use and manipulate. All the force has to do is enter your auric field through this "hole" in your mind-pattern. To close the holes and correct the mind-pattern, it is important to find out what in your life is controlling you so that you can stop it.

What controls you? Is it a person? Anyone who "pulls your strings" or "pushes your buttons" is controlling you. Anyone who you allow to put you down, or who makes you feel like less of a person is controlling you. When you react to their manipulation, you are not in control. The other person controls you. This could be a parent, spouse, child, relative, co-worker, or neighbor, for example.

Do your emotions control you? When emotions are out of balance, they can create their own subpersonalities. Each emotion has its own color, tone, and archetype within your auric field. Anger is comprised of the color red, Fear is yellow, Jealousy is green. Every time you have experience these emotions without passing them up to your Oversoul, the energy of these specific subpersonalities are fed. Anger gets stronger, Fear gets stronger, Jealousy gets stronger. Now, *they* are in control of *you*. You can make all the promises you want, but what happens when your buttons get pushed? All of a sudden, Anger is controlling you, or Fear, or Jealousy. You have lost the battle. Your emotions are in control.

Perhaps it is illness that controls you. Do you need that illness in order to feel important, or as a way to get attention and/or love? Do you have chronic health issues that never seem to go away? Or you just get rid of something and something else pops up to take its place? What part of you needs and allows this type of control?

Do alcohol and drugs control you? How about tobacco? Sex? There are support groups for alcoholism, drug, and sex addiction; for people who cannot stop shopping, gambling, and/or shoplifting. There are support groups for people controlled by bulimia, anorexia, obsessive compulsive disorder. You name it, it is out there controlling somebody, somewhere. Is it controlling you?

Does food control you? Food controlling you does not imply that you are overweight. Could you go a day without chocolate or sugar? Could you fast for 24 hours without anything but water? Most likely you would not starve to death and die...so could you??

How about fashion? Are you the first to get the latest clothing, hairstyles, home décor, without thinking if you even like them or not? How about cars, motorcycles, trucks, motor vehicles, boat...the list is endless.

Or fads, be it body-piercing, tattoos, or acquiring all kinds of doodads and knickknacks that will be useless practically before you even have them out of the box. Do you have to have whatever everyone else has?

Plastic surgery controls people. They keep going back and redoing every part of the body until there is nothing left to redo. Then they start over again.

Some people start exercising and cannot stop. They exercise continually and constantly, sometimes building up muscle masses that would put Hercules to shame. Others exercise until they do not have a drop of fat on their bodies, then begin destroying their muscle tissues, ligaments, and internal organs.

Do your experiences use and control you, or do you use and control your experiences? This is the bottom line. If anything or anyone controls you in any way, shape, or form, you are a prime candidate for mass and/or individual mind-control. When you are in control of your own self, no one and no thing can control you. Everything in moderation is acceptable, but when something takes over your life to the degree where it controls you, you create a mind-pattern that says "outside forces can and do control me."

This leaves holes in your mind-pattern and auric field that tells anyone who can understand this information that you are a perfect candidate for mind-control. Learn to breathe yourself into your center. Identify the strong aspects of your mind-pattern and the ones that need strengthening. Anchor yourself in the strength of your own Oversoul and God-Mind. Take control over absolutely anything that has control over you, remembering to keep the balance. You can be pulled off-center in every way imaginable, and you will be. These are your tests.

Be the monitor of your own progress. The more you use internal monitors, the less chance outside monitors can step in to do the job for you. Whenever you let your guard down, there will be somebody or something that will knowingly and gladly push you out of your center.

Part of your reason for existing in physical reality is to find out who and what you are. Being pushed out of your center tells you who you are not. Operating from outside of your center allows others to define you according to their terms. They can mold and bend you like clay to create the person that they need for their own purposes. You are so busy molding and bending that you do not have time to recognize what is happening to you.

Only when you stand firm in your center, in control of absolutely every aspect of your life, are all the holes of your mind-pattern completely sealed shut. When this happens, no one or no thing can control you. But even when the door is closed to outsiders, remember that they will still come knocking. It is up to you to ensure that they do not enter.

Earth's Mind-Pattern

Most people realize that the energy of the Earth varies from place to place. What they do not stop to realize is that the planet Earth, as a living, breathing, sentient entity, has a mind-pattern that affects its energy field.

Whatever emanates from the mind-pattern of the Earth attracts that kind of experience to it. You are here because the Earth has the mind-pattern to attract you. You are a part of the Earth's experience for its growth. You are a reflection for the Earth in whatever location you choose to reside upon it.

The Earth's mind-pattern creates its archetypes and auric field. You can view the Earth's auric field in the same that you view a person's auric field. Where its field is dark and negative, it attracts beings and/or experiences with the same energy. In actuality, the templates for these experiences already exist, rising up from the Earth itself. The beings merely come in to help the template created by the Earth's mind-pattern fulfill itself.

Depending upon the template, this attracts different aspects of physical reality to fulfill it. For example, perhaps the template from one place looks like a castle, so the castle is built to fulfill the template. There might also be a template for a moat, and the specific types of vegetation. There will also be a template for the type of person to inhabit the castle, and for the experiences the person will have. The person, vegetation, moat, and castle are all outpicturings of the Earth's mind-pattern in that locale.

Just as you attract your experiences to you, the Earth attracts its experiences to itself. Where the Earth has a "negative" in its mind-pattern, the template in that area is a negative one and attracts negative experiences. This might be a manufacturer of toxic materials. Then, if the Earth does not correct its mind-pattern, a toxic spill may occur, representing damage to the physical body of the Earth.

This is the equivalent of a human with a negative mind-pattern that exits in the auric field. First, the person attracts the mental and emotional support for that mind-pattern, either positive or negative. Then, the next step is for the mind-pattern to settle into the physical body. A toxic spill on the Earth is equivalent to a cancer in a person's body.

This is where most people stop. They get ensconced in a pattern of behavior and stay there. They attract experiences to hold them where they are. They are pulled to specific areas of the Earth's consciousness to support their current state of being. In the same way, the Earth pulls to itself people that support its current state of consciousness. Between the pull of the Earth's energy and that of the people, everyone gets stuck without upward movement or growth.

For the Earth, this expresses somewhere in its body. For example, it releases these suppressed emotions as an earthquake, volcanic eruption, tidal wave, hurricane, etc. This is similar to the way a person expresses his/her suppressed negative experiences and emotions. When a person suppresses internal angers, depending upon the source of the anger, he/she may experience an accident, such as an explosion, fire, drowning, broken bone, etc. These experiences are all outpicturing some part of the mind-pattern.

When the Earth becomes volatile and changes, then the beings originally attracted to it, in turn, must change or leave. This sometimes means physical death. When the mind-pattern of the Earth no longer supports a person, the person unconsciously and automatically leaves.

This is an interconnected universe. The mind-pattern that exists within you can attract or repel disease, bacteria, microorganisms, parasites, etc. To these micro-bugs, your physical body represents their world. They are born, live, and die right inside your physical body. The consciousness that your living organism exudes is what attracts or repels them to or from you. Once inside your body, they live out their purpose and existence.

When your mind-pattern changes, they must change. Either they adjust, or their consciousness leaves, i.e., death, and they move onto other places. Your body contains worlds within worlds. Your body exudes an energy field that is a template for other species to fulfill. These templates exist for everything from the type of food and clothing that can come into your auric field to the type of people who can enter it and be a part of your world.

This is the same for all parts of your physical body. Because it operates as one, you may forget that the physical body is actually a compilation of many consciousness. Each cell has its own consciousness. Together, enough cells with the same mind-pattern are drawn together to form a kidney or a lung. The kidney has a separate consciousness, the lung has a separate consciousness, etc. You can speak to these individual consciousness. Or you can break it down even further and speak to the individualized cell consciousness that create the group consciousness. But remember, they all merely fulfill the mind-pattern that exudes from you. They exist within the world that you created for them. Again, worlds within worlds exist within you.

Continue to extrapolate this concept into the Earth. The Earth holds worlds within worlds. Everything that exists on the planet fulfills the template that the Earth sends out via its mind-pattern. Negative experiences take place where a negative part of the Earth's mind-pattern exists. Filth, poverty, crime, desolation, etc. exist in areas of the Earth's mind-pattern that support this. Positive experiences occur where a positive part of the Earth's mind-pattern exists. Abundance, health, prosperity, well-being, etc. exist in areas of the Earth's mind-patterns that support this.

This is why physically relocating can make a difference in who and what you are. You can move to a place on the Earth that pulls you down, holds you where you are, or supports your upward and inward growth. You may be able to function in a place that pulls you down, but it takes a lot of energy to do this. There really is not any time to spare. Go to a place on the Earth that supports who and what you are. Some people will choose to stay in the negative energy places to help those out that need to leave. They will sacrifice their physical bodies for their choices, but in doing so their soul will grow exponentially.

Evolution means that one consciousness has to change to change the next consciousness. Who will change first? Will it be a conscious, directed, focused change, or a spontaneous change that occurs on the unconscious levels to force a change?

One consciousness changing means change for all interconnected ones. Even the smallest step on the upward spiral changes everything in some way. As the Earth cleans up its consciousness, it will attract balanced experiences to itself. In the same way, when you clean up your consciousness, you attract balanced experiences to yourself.

Develop a conscious awareness of all of the effects of your choices - including where you choose to live and why. Ask your Oversoul if it is time to relocate, and if so, where. Allow yourself the energy boost that the mind-pattern of the Earth can provide to help propel you faster and easier toward your own internal goals.

One Mind-Pattern=Global Control

Each continent of the world has its own specific feeling, or frequency. From there, think about the different countries, states, and regions. Each area has its own unique feeling, or frequency, and as such, attracts individuals that match that particular frequency.

Each region has different clothing, customs, money, foods, songs, dances, and spiritual traditions. Soul-personalities are attracted to specific regions because these regions match their frequencies and mind-patterns. Even the languages and dialects are specific to certain areas. This is because the tones that are spoken reflect and affect mind-patterns and cellular structure. There is an all-pervading reason for these differences.

Whenever you choose to travel, you enjoy the differences from region to region, area to area. These differences provide you with entertainment as well as specific effects on your physical, mental, and emotional bodies, or, your overall frequency.

This diversity is slowly dissipating with careful planning. Languages are all assimilating slowly, slowly, into the one global language of English. Monies are being integrated into one global currency. Every town world wide, large or small, is getting a McDonald's, Wendy's, and a Burger King.

Small business is quietly being targeted. Take the office supply business as one example. There used to be a myriad of small office supply stores. Then stores like Staples, Office Depot, and Office Max appeared on the scene. Small business could not compete, and many had to close their doors. Now, Staples, Office Depot, and Office Max are having financial difficulties. Soon, one or two of these giants will bow out of the market, and there will be only one and possibly two places to get office supplies.

This scenario occurs over and over, one industry at a time. Even in agriculture, small farmers are slowly being replaced by corporate industry. It is becoming less and less feasible for people to go into business for themselves. Just opening up a business banking account takes a mountain of paperwork. Large bank customers have a different set of rules than small bank customers, regardless of the official rules. When everyone is working nine to five, there is much less chance of taking creativity away from the group mind-pattern and funneling it into individual creativity.

Employee benefits and taxes paid by small businesses are consuming more and more of their profit margin. Unable to compete and/or comply with complex and expensive state and federal laws, they cease to exist, leaving only large, faceless bureaucratic organizations that take on a depersonalized and desensitized view of the individual.

In these ways, individuality and diversity is slowly dissipating. One town looks like the next, one region is becoming more and more similar to the others, and every individual is becoming more and more like the next one.

Everyone is watching the same shows, going to the same movies, listening to the same music. Everyone is beginning to dress alike, drive the same vehicles, eat the same food, use the same money, shop at the same stores, dine at the same restaurants. Everyone's expectations are falling into line with that of the next person.

Now, throw in emotional upheaval and get everyone's thoughts flowing in the same direction. There have been enough government-generated studies on physical and emotional health to know how the public will react when given a certain set of circumstances. They know what fear and fright do to people. They know how they will respond. There is not a doubt in their minds.

One mind-pattern is much easier to control and manipulate. Most animals operate with a group mind, commonly referred to as a "herd mentality" because most have not yet realized their individualized mind. Whatever one animal does, the others will automatically follow, without thinking. Creating a "herd" mentality among humans is the most effective way to control them.

Why are national anthems, "I love America" songs, and American flags suddenly showing up with every blink of the eye? Why was CNN reporting that 7 out of 10 Americans were depressed, 1 out of 3 could not sleep, and 1 out of 2 Americans were "confused?" Were you? Or is this what was trying to be created?

What was happening up in the air while all the aircraft was on the ground after the recent targeting of the WTC? Could more satellites have been made operational and more ELF bombarded upon the unsuspecting populace to feed the already unsettled emotions?

Is the global community being manipulated into a war they do not want? Do you want your children and loved ones going off to war? Do you want poverty stricken countries filled with people who only want shelter and enough food to eat bombed and destroyed because of the acts of a malicious few? Do you want to live in a military state because you are willing to live your life in fear? Do you want an "Office of the Homeland?"

Are you in control of your own mind-pattern or is someone controlling it for you? Look at the circumstances around yourself and make your own decisions. Choose to live your life in freedom. Think before you act, but always remember,

whatever is NOT in your mind-pattern cannot happen to you.

Maintain individuality. You may think that you will not be caught up in it, but you may not have a choice. If everyone has a flag on his/her car and you do not, you eventually may have to put one up or become a target yourself. Now is the time to make your statement before that time comes.

Patriotism vs. Warmongering

Many people feel like they need to "do something" in response to the recent domestic incidents. Because they do not know exactly what that is, they are doing what the media is telling them to do. The public is being fed a steady diet of mind-control called "patriotism." American flags are displayed everywhere, from front yards and windows, to cars, trucks, buses, and billboards. Three major networks preempted regular programming for a charity benefit. Music stations are playing "I Love America" songs in rapid succession. Relief efforts exist in every town, incorporating all available citizens from school children to adults.

The media is feeding people a constant diet of "stand up and fight" for your freedoms. However, your freedoms are not being attacked by outsiders. Your freedoms are being asked for by your official leaders, and people everywhere are responding by willingly handing it over to them. The powers-that-be are winning their own internal war. The situation was created, and now, as always, the people are reacting like frightened sheep looking for a shepherd to protect them.

Patriotism is a good thing - uniting together to promote unity and harmony. Feeling good about where you live is important. Feeling like you are a part of the whole is great. Warmongering is another thing.

People are being bombarded, whether they want to be or not, with the threat of terrorist attacks. People are being instructed to go airports two hours in advance of departure, but are reporting that other than the time spent, the present process is not that different from the past. Security checks are everywhere. People are beginning to feel a "militaristic" flavor to the country. Air marshals on flights, national guardsmen and women on duty, security checkpoints at airports, an official "Office of the Homeland."

There are reports of pilots and passengers not wanting to fly because of dark-skinned people on their flights; of entire families being asked to leave planes. These people are being targeted, separated, and segregated. What does this remind you of?

Middle Eastern peoples are being targeted, but you really do not know by whom. When good people are hurt, other good people get frightened. Perhaps they will be taken away for their own safety? What good family would not want to protect their children from attacks against them because of the color of their skin? And then what will happen to them? Who will know? Who will care? And, who will be next? Divide and conquer.

Hysteria is being perpetuated whether you want it or not. A feeling of nervousness is pervading the country. News reports continue to tell the American people that terrorist attacks "will happen again." There is not a doubt in anyone's mind - the only doubt, for those who are willing to question, is who is really behind these attacks and why?

As long as every area of the country gets attacked in one way or another, warmongering, in the form of "patriotism" will be promoted. The collective unconscious will be revved up to "seek and destroy" the supposed perpetrators, until they will willingly send their sons and daughters marching off to war to protect your "freedoms."

As with all things, it is best not to feed the cycles. Anger going out means anger coming in. Like attracts like. Feed the cycle, and you become part of the cycle. Your choice. Making a gigantic production and show of strength as our honest citizens are sent to the Middle East to look for a bunch of ragtag rebels is ridiculous. This is a great public display designed to garner support for handing over your freedoms. Unfortunately, this is supported by well-meaning people filled with honest intent.

In addition, the United States is sending millions of dollars to Afghanistan as "humanitarian aid." Who do you think is going to wind up with the medical supplies and food? The general populace, or their freedom fighters? The Afghanistan people will want to make sure that their protectors are taken care of first. Will this shorten the "war" or make it less painful? The media is reporting that this will be a "long and sustained" war. Why does it have to be?

Precautions are always in order, whether you are on an airplane, or if you decide to walk down the street. Everyone should always use caution. You do not want to stand in front of a moving bus, and declare that it will not hit you. Keep your eyes open, and step aside. Paranoia is another thing. Every time you see a bus on the street, do not run and hide. Stay out of the street, and most likely it will not hit you. See it coming, step out of the way. Use your judgment.

Being angry, argumentative, and aggressive will only attract these things to you. Sending "light, love, and peace" is not the answer either. Whether you like it or not, this world is your dream, it is your reflection of you. You could not exist within this world if there was not some part of you that created it. Therefore, clean up your own house, literally and figuratively speaking, so that your world reflects that. You can make this world a better place by making yourself a better space.

As that occurs, your world, including this planet has to change to reflect your inner changes. This is Universal Law—the outer reflects the inner and the inner reflects the outer. Simple, direct, and extremely practical. Stop sending "peace, love, and light" to others when you are the one that needs it the most. Send it to yourself. Balance your own inner qualities. Find your own mind-pattern holes. Criticizing and judging others is only a reflection of how you view yourself.

The only safe place is you. It is not a geographical location.

You are being forced into your own strength and fortitude. You will find out what you are capable of, one way or the other. Develop your ability to be proactive, even if it is an uncomfortable journey within. Rather than "seek and destroy" in the outer world, "seek and reformulate" what already exists within. You can rapidly change the outer world by rapidly doing what you need to do. Stop procrastinating, self-sabotaging, and creating blocks just because you know how. Internalize your focus. Implant the collective unconscious with a new path to follow. *You can make a difference today!*

Simultaneous Existence

Think of your life as a diamond with yourself in the center. Looking from the inside out, every facet that you see could conceivably represent another life, separate, yet existing at the same time. Each facet touches other facets, all interconnected and necessary for the whole.

Where one facet meets another, there is a blending of experience— that meeting point is important for the whole to exist. That one meeting place belongs to both facets, one influencing the other, while helping to maintain the integrity of separate experiences.

Now, imagine that diamond in a room surrounded by mirrors, where the diamond is replicated an infinite number of times. Each time it is replicated, more and more facets appear, each one connected to another, each one an extension of the facets surrounding it.

Looking from the inside out, the number of facets that you see appear endless.

Each facet can represent a simultaneous life. Each one is a reflection of your soul, each one is a reflection in someway of every facet, or life, that it touches. For example, someone who is a prisoner in one facet may wear stripes in this facet as his/her connection. He/she may be in a prison in the jungles of Africa, or in a high-profile political prison in a developed country. In another facet he/she may create a prison-like environment. This could be a body that does not function properly, so that the body becomes a prison. It could be a spouse or relative who allows little freedom. It could be agoraphobia – fear of everything. It could be fear of travel. The list is as long as your imagination.

These facets all represent a person who is a prisoner – sometimes imprisoned by others, sometimes by the body, sometimes by the mind. These facets, or lives, answer these questions in God-Mind: What is it like to be a prisoner? How many ways can it be experienced? What is it like to be free? What is it like not to be free?

Careers are replicated as well. Think about a scientist and the endless possibilities that this theme could be repeated and experienced. Or an artist. Or a medical professional. Relationships, finances, religions, etc. All are multidimensional in the true experience of the soul.

God-Mind explores all things and all possibilities. For example, you could imagine God-Mind as consisting of one section with science, one with healing, one with physics, etc. Within each section, there are an infinite number of soul-personalities exploring that subject in all ways in every dimension conceivable and beyond. Remember, there is ONE SOUL and everything is an extension of that ONE SOUL. All soul-personalities simply represent the various segments of God-Mind exploring Itself.

It does not matter if it takes many souls to accomplish this, or only one. Every physical body in this reality can only contain a certain amount of soul energy. Some physical bodies, for example, contain less soul energy than others. These types of physical bodies are comparatively more dense.

You can determine this for yourself quite simply. Use your consciousness to "weigh" the soul energy present in any body. Create an old-fashioned balancing scale by using your pineal gland as the center and your hands as the weighing tables. Envision the frequency of anyone you know. Feel the frequency of the soul-personality and also of the physical structure. Use your hands to "weigh" the density of the physical body. Then, use your hands to weigh the density of the soul energy present in the body.

You will need to repeat this exercise several times to get a grasp of comparative weights. Discover for yourself that the denser physical structures contain less soul energy while the lighter physical structures contain more soul energy. Do not let your eyes fool you. Physical weight is not important – look for the density of the cellular structure.

People sitting around a table will automatically create balance in this way. Unconsciously, they will arrange themselves so that the overall soul energy present is always balanced. You may see this when two people with less soul energy will sit across the table from one person with the equivalent soul energy of the two people. Do not judge, but do observe what is happening, moving your consciousness as necessary to study and learn for yourself. God-Mind always maintains balance within Itself, one way or another.

You can acquire more soul energy as the physical body becomes less dense and the cellular structure becomes cleaner. When this happens, the cells vibrate more quickly, and the Oversoul responds by pouring in more soul energy. Envision the energy structure above your head as a funnel. Label "Self" at the bottom, "Oversoul" in the middle, and "God-

Mind" at the top. Visualize how your Oversoul simply pours in more soul energy as the body can hold more.

Sometimes, when the portion of soul energy poured into "Self" is large enough, you may experience a soul merger. This can be when an entire soul-personality from within your own Oversoul is merged with the existing one, or it could simply be more Oversoul energy. When a true merger occurs, the existing soul-personality expands and changes.

Without guidance, some people may think that they are going crazy. They may experience different realities focusing in and out, not know simple things like how to tell time and directions to places that should be familiar. They may even have trouble recognizing some people who the "old" soul-personality knows, but who the newly merged soul-personality does not yet consciously know.

Some people mistake this experience for a walk-in, which is entirely different. A walk-in exists when another soul-personality from another Oversoul takes over a body. A walk-in is rarely allowed under Universal Law, because it involves one frequency operating the physical structure of another frequency. This is comparative to channeling, but worse for the host's physical structure. This means that the host's physical structure will begin to break down and have a variety of health issues, severe enough that the usual eventual consequence is death of the host body.

Is it important to know simultaneous existences that influence you now? Again, the answer is to spend your resources wisely. Sometimes it is important to understand how a specific mind-pattern came into being, why it is so strong, and why it holds you there. Understanding other life lines can be beneficial, but it can also be detrimental.

For instance, perhaps your soul-personality needs to work something out with someone, but when you remember a great or lost love, you may forsake your current work to try to recreate the other life line. Sometimes you meet people that you recognize from other life lines that have no recollection of you and no desire for you to be a part of their lives.

That is because they are focused here instead of "there." You may find other life lines more attractive and luring because it provides an escape from this reality. As mentioned in "Knowing By Knowing," sometimes NOT knowing is a blessing, allowing you focus on this present life line so that your soul-personality can accomplish whatever needs to be done.

Memories from other life lines can provide an activation that can change the course of events in this one. This can be either positive or negative, depending upon how you deal with it.

Only you can decide for yourself if you want to investigate your other life lines. Sometimes, your conscious mind has no choice when it is thrust before you. Whatever your decisions, make them in awareness. Ask your Oversoul to guide and strengthen you so that you can deal with and handle whatever information is presented. You may go in search of one thing and find something entirely different. Allow the journey, whatever it is, wherever it takes you, in your multidimensional inner exploration of Self, Oversoul, and God-Mind.

Index

Expansions Ordering Information

PO Box 12 St. Joseph, MI 49085
Phone (616) 429-8615   Fax(616) 429-8616
website www.stewartswerdlow.com

BOOKS BY STEWART

Blue Blood, True Blood: Conflict & Creation $25
Based on his personal experience, including his recent targeting by an Illuminati agent, Stewart discusses the true history of this galaxy, solar system, and the planet Earth; how the Illuminati began; what their plans are for society and the Earth based on his intricate personal involvement; and how the N.W.O. is using mind-control to herd people toward their goal. A must-read, fascinating account that will change your belief system forever!

The Healers Handbook: A Journey Into Hyperspace (Sky Books) $22
A comprehensive book never before accomplished on this planet, including chapters on color therapy, deciphering hyperspace sentences, archetype dictionary, unconventional healing techniques, dream analysis, dream dictionary, time travel, communicating with the departed, prayer, meditation, visualization exercises, much more. Unlock DNA sequences preprogrammed within you since the beginning of your existence. A must-have, easy-to-use reference and healing guide for every personal and professional library. You will never be the same!

Montauk: The Alien Connection (Sky Books) $20
An autobiographical account of Stewart's amazing life adventures, giving the reader personal insight into this unique and multi-talented man.

The White Owl Legends: An Archetypal Story of Creation $20
By Agnes & Chief White Owl. Interpreted by Stewart Swerdlow. The energy of Chief White Owl dictated these legends to Spiritualist trance medium Agnes over sixty years ago. Indians are descendants of the Atlans, a group of beings from the Pleiades who colonized Atlantis. Includes how the alien races seeded the original Earth population.

Forthcoming books - Dream Dictionary; Mind-Pattern Analysis

BOOKS BY JANET

IN SEARCH OF YOURSELF SERIES
Includes: Exercises, Meditations, Visualizations, Affirmations. Glossary, Index
Book 1: The Beginning
Learn the basics of auric fields, meditation, releasing the past, Oversoul communication, growing younger, becoming your own teacher. **$15**
Book 2: Moving Forward
Learn objective observation and listening, releasing judgment/criticism of Self, how to change, define habit responses, establishing vertical growth. **$15**
Book 3: Finding The Balance
Learn to identify sub-personalities, become proactive, "predict" the future,

The Little Fluff Children's Books Series
- **Book 1: Auras**   • **Book 2: Chakras**
- **Book 3: Archetypes**   • **Book 4 Protection**

An easy-to-follow teaching format that builds strong, aware minds right from the start. Ages 3-6, **$12.95** each, **$9.95** two or more.

Belief Systems Shattered

A compilation of Janet's articles from the Expansions website. Simple, direct, and easy to read, this book explores many trendy New Age topics, challenging the reader to question personal decisions and direction, from, is love the answer, vegetarianism, name changing, channeling, Oversouls, and good and evil, to mind-control, sleepers, and the Illuminati, with many other topics in between. Janet writes what many people are already thinking. **$25**

Practical Tips For Everyday Living

52 weeks, 365 days, from the Expansions website, with a different theme each week, including such timely topics as abundance, anger, aura cleaning, compassion, depression, DNA activation, fear, identifying freqencies, know by knowing, proactive, releasing, rejuvenation, victim mentality, vision, and weight. Excellent information and insight! **$15**

Life Support Group™ Leader Manual $25
Life Support Group™ Children's Classes Manual $25
Life Support Group™ Youth Classes Manual $25

Audio Tape   Meditation Tape: Into The Silence By Janet Swerdlow

Includes three keys for successful meditation; learn to know by knowing; move through the veils between the conscious, subconscious, and super conscious minds. **$10**

VIDEOS

New! Dream Analysis & Color Codes
In-depth exploration of dreams, including symbolism, mind-patterns, soul-purpose, and healing. Use of color codes to unlock the mind-pattern, create/layer color codes for mental/physical healing, contact God-Mind and Oversoul, add depth to prayer, deep space travel, personal frequencies correlated to the Angelic Hierarchy. 4 Tapes, 6-7 hours, vinyl binder. **$130**.

New! Simultaneous Existence
Move beyond the linear concept of reincarnation and time. Access your multi-dimensional self via Angelic/Oversoul contact, understand walk-ins and mergers, DNA, bleed-throughs, Delta-T antenna, simultaneity syndromes, dreaming, astral travel, out-of-body experiences, contacting Angelic Hierachy for specific help, personal Angels. 4 tapes, 6-7 hours, vinyl binder. **$130**.

New! The Montauk Project Symposium 2001
For the first time ever, Montauk Project survivors Stewart Swerdlow (a/k/a "Stan Cambell"), Duncan Cameron, with researcher Peter Moon share the same stage at the Lightgate Center in Thetford, Vermont. Symposium topics include: Alien involvement, Genetic Manipulation, Illuminati, Nazi, & Occult connection, Mind-Control, History, Positive Side, Technology, Time Travel. Fascinating!
- **Part I**, 8 hours, 4 tapes, vinyl binder **$125**.
- **Part II**, 8 hours, 4 tapes, vinyl binder **$125** • **Part I & II**, (set) **$225**

- **The Best of The Montauk Project Symposium 2001**, 4 hours, 2 tapes, vinyl binder **$75**
- **Illuminati & The Montauk Project with Stewart Swerdlow**, 2 1/2 hours, 1 Tape **$35**
- **Synchronicity & The Occult with Peter Moon**, 2 1/2 hours, 1 tape **$35**
- **Montauk Psychics with Duncan Cameron**, 2 1/2 hours, 1 tape **$35**
- **Belief Systems Shattered with Janet Swerdlow**, 2 1/2 hours, 1 tape, **$35**
- **Current Events with Stewart Swerdlow, 2 1/2 hours**, 1 tape, **$35**

Language of Hyperspace
Stewart's base seminar for all the others. He explains in detail the Original language that emanates from the Mind of God consisting of color, tone, and archetype. This intraspecies, interuniversal language is used by all beings. 4 tapes, 6-7 hours, vinyl binder. **$130**

DNA, Galactic History & You!
Learn how to open and analyze your own genetic structure. Understand who and what you really are. See your true origins and learn the true history of the Earth and the experiment of humankind. 4 tapes, 6-7 hours, vinyl binder. **$130**

How I Became A Hyperspace Healer
Stewart discusses his background, initiation into the healing arts, and his experiences with unusual forces that molded his character and shaped his life. 60 minutes. **$25**

Basic & Intermediate Color Therapy
Includes orientation to the Language of Hyperspace, T-Bar, cleansing breaths, chakra spinning. Uses of the following colors: brown, pale red, pale orange, pale yellow, medium green, ice blue, royal blue, violet, silver, gold, black, white, copper, purple, maroon, turquoise, and pink. Applications, examples, and meditative demonstrations. 4 tapes, 6-7 hours, vinyl binder. **$130**

Triad Healing
Basic healing archetypes, name frequencies, colors, pineal gland, sweeping/ sealing the crown chakra. Intermediate healing techniques, turning back the clock, raising hertz levels, affirmations, charging water, Angelic help. Hyperspace surgery, unusual techniques. 4 tapes, 6-7 hours, vinyl binder. **$130**

Illuminating the Illuminati
Cutting edge information on subjects never before publicly discussed by Stewart. Hear how he was triggered once again by an Illuminati agent and found his way back. Stewart describes the true formation of the history of this galaxy, solar system, and planet, and how the Illuminati came into being. Hear what their plans are for you and your future. Time is of the essence. Not for tree huggers! 3 hours, tow tapes, vinyl binder. **$60**

New! Level II Survivor or Surpasser
For the serious student only. Learn the difference between merely surviving a victim mentality, or surpassing it. After a brief review of basic hyperspace techniques, you will learn tools to remove victim mentality from yourself as well as help others do the same. In this seminar you will learn to: Define, Identify & Release Victim Mentality, Understand Victimization Framework, Utilize Personal Protection Techniques, Use Lion Frequency/Color Codes, Use Merger & Infinity Archetypes, Open Immortality DNA Sequences, Increase Personal & Physical Power, Understand Reptilian Brain Fight or Flight Syndrome, Identify Your God-Self, Follow Through with Perfection of Self. This 6 tape series, over 12 hours long, is only available to those students who have taken and successfully passed the Level I certification test, also available on-line. **$195**.

All prices subject to change without notice. Contact us for current pricing and S&H charges.

SERVICES

Name Analysis
Using your birth name, Stewart combines his knowledge of archetypes, numerology, and colors to reveal pertinent birth information, such as traits and characteristics with which you were born, mind-patterns that can be enhanced or need to be corrected. Includes number and color codes to unlock hidden DNA sequences and buried memories.

Personality Profile
Using your birth name, frequency, birth date, and place of residence, Stewart provides an in-depth comprehensive 8-10 page report which includes information about your basic traits and characteristics, health issues, relationships, residence, DNA/simultaneous experiences, color and number codes, future choices/suggestions, and a detailed summary.

Dream Analysis
Because you spend 1/3 of your earthly life in the dream state, discover The Language of Hyperspace that speaks to you through your dreams.

Radionic Treatments Call for details.

Personal Template
Stewart creates a unique 3 x 5 template for a specific life issue for use on your radionic machine, to place under your pillow wile sleeping, or to wear around your neck.

Personal Archetype
Receive an 8 x 10 color drawing of your hyperspace signature, your unique symbol that represents the totality of your current mind-pattern, along with an analysis of the symbol and its meaning to your life. Includes 30 minute consultation.

Residential Frequency Analysis
Using your current address, Stewart combines his knowledge of archetypes, numerology, and colors to reveal pertinent residential information, such as the energies associated with the building, street, town, state, and country in which you live. Also provides color codes for decoration and enhancing personal energy. Thinking of changing your current residence? Additional address discount.

Crime-Solving
Individual or public law enforcement.

Alternative Business Consulting
For business start-ups, current, expansions.
Services/Pricing Development, Marketing/Promotional Advice, Current Business Review, Goal Development, Business Planning, Record keeping, Organization, Seminar/Workshop/Lecture Development, Public Speaking Coaching, Mind-Pattern Analysis Related To You Business, Office Layout/ Colors, Business Location/Relocation, Manuscript Review, Editing.

Brochure/Services/Pricing Development
Includes two-sided, three-fold 8 1/2 x 11 brochure.

Business Card Development Ready for printing.

Business Logos
Based upon your personal archetypes and type of business, a logo is developed to promote prosperity, harmony, and direction. Also includes interpretation/ adjustment of current logos. Provided on computer disc.

Co-Publishing Opportunities
Exciting opportunities to publish written works. Manuscript review, editing, layout, book covers. **Call for details.**

Contact us for pricing details.

STEWART'S SEMINARS

The certificate program enables qualified students to legally teach **Swerdlow Hyperspace Techniques.**™
Level I
The Language of Hyperspace
The original language that emanates from the Mind of God consisting of Color, tone, and archetype. Intraspecies, interuniversal language used by all beings.

Triad Healing
Elevate healing methods to the next level using colors, tone, and archetype.

Intermediate Color Codes, & Archetypes/ Simultaneous Existence
Use color codes to unlock sections of your mind-pattern. Move beyond the scope of linear time to explore your personal connections to the realm where time and space do not exist.
Review & certification.

Level II

Survivor or Surpassor?
Break down the victim mentality into its minute components. Create methods to remove them.

Plants/Animals/Places
Understand and connect to the overall group mind and/or energy center to incorporate the particular energies and use them for specific reasons.

Scanning
Hands-on and minds-on people, places, and things to "know." Learn how to manipulate the energy fields for a higher purpose.
Review & certification.

Level III

Support Structure/Thought Bands/Manifestations
All three of the above courses provide a detailed look at the intricate layers/levels of the physical structure based on personal experiences and thought-patterns.
Review & certification.

Level IV

In-depth Healing Practicum/Research Project
Participants will bring in subjects for healing work/research in the following categories: babies, elderly, mentally/physically challenged, or other categories subject to approval. Participants will decide on a course of healing under Stewart's direct supervision. Mind-patterns of clients and caretakers will be evaluated, applicable environments will be reviewed, medical records/documentation must be provided.
Review & certification.

Certification Test, Level I
For the serious student who wishes to verify his/her knowledge of the Swerdlow Hyperspace Techniques™. This test can be taken after all Level I seminars are completed, or after all of the Level I video series have been viewed: The Language of Hyperspace, DNA, Galactic History, & You, Triad Healing, Simultaneous Existence, Dream Analysis & Intermediate Color Codes. The test consists of basic information that you need to know in order to adequately understand the next level in the series. A certificate of completion will be issued upon satisfactory completion of the test. **$95**

JANET'S SEMINARS

Activating Your Inner Mystic Part I
Easily connect with the mystic within through the Language of Feeling. Recognize and understand what you are already doing. By building on that knowledge utilizing basic metaphysical principles, you will discover that your abilities are truly limitless!

Activating Your Inner Mystic Part II
Deepen your ability for multidimensional communication using the Language of Feeling. Strengthen the metaphysical principles that bind all hidden knowledge. Understand how close you are to the answers you seek, and why they seemingly elude you.

Activating Your Inner Mystic Part III
What do you teach others? No matter where you are in your life, you are a constant example of something. People learn from you on a daily basis. Make conscious decisions of what you want to teach and how. Focus on your leadership abilities to strengthen relationships, career, finances, and personal satisfaction. Upon completion of this course, you will be certified to be a Life Support Group™ team leader, if you choose.

Seminars available for children, youth, young adult, and adults.

Life Support Groups™
Based on Janet's *IN SEARCH OF YOURSELF SERIES*
You are your own best teacher!

Explore:	the most fascinating person you know: YOU!
Develop:	inner sight, intuition, Oversoul communication, leadership abilities.
Change:	self, relationships, career, finances, home.
Interpret:	your inner life to change your outer life, and your outer life to change your inner life.
Learn:	discernment.
Understand:	mysticism, God-Mind, spirituality, positive/negative, universal/psychic energy, color/sound/archetype, Oversoul communication, other realities, simultaneous existence, vertical/horizontal growth.
Tools:	group wisdom, toning, meditation, visualization, prayer affirmations, stretching exercises, mental exercises, Oversoul communication.
Result:	learn to easily find your own answers.

Become a Life Support Group™ leader or member in your community.